More praise for *American Destiny and the Calling of the Church*

"This book argues passionately and persuasively that the church needs to be a 'sentinel church' to guard the biblical vision of unity, justice, and harmony against political and religious distortions. Artfully referencing a wide range of historical and theological resources, Paul Wee draws on his own deeply rooted evangelical faith, his authentic patriotism, and his decades of experience as a global church leader to make this urgent plea and to provide this stimulating starting point for the debate."

> —*William E. Lesher, President Emeritus, Lutheran School of Theology at Chicago: Chair, Board of Trustees, Council for a Parliament of the World's Religions*

"Dr. Wee invites us to engage in an ongoing debate about the relevancy of the gospel proclaimed by the church in a fractured and wounded world."

> —*Rev. Dr Ishmael Noko, LWF General Secretary*

See www.lutheranvoices.com

American Destiny
and the Calling of the Church

Paul A. Wee

Augsburg Fortress
Minneapolis

AMERICAN DESTINY AND THE CALLING OF THE CHURCH

Large-quantity purchases or custom editions of these books are available at a discount from
the publisher. For more information, contact the sales department at Augsburg Fortress,
Publishers, 1-800-328-4648, or write to: Sales Director, Augsburg Fortress, Publishers, P.O.
Box 1209, Minneapolis, MN 55440-1209.

Editor: David Lott

Cover Design: © Koechel Peterson and Associates, Inc., Minneapolis, MN
          www.koechelpeterson.com

Cover photo: Royalty-Free/Corbis. Used by permission.

Library of Congress Cataloging-in-Publication Data
Wee, Paul A., 1937-
  American destiny and the calling of the church / Paul A. Wee.
      p. cm. — (Lutheran voices)
  Includes bibliographical references.
  ISBN 0-8066-8002-4 (pbk. : alk. paper)
  1. Church and state—United States. 2. United States—Foreign relations—2001- I. Title.
II. Series.
  BR516.W433 2006
  261.70973—dc22   2005037191

Manufactured in the U. S.A.

10   09   08   07   06   1   2   3   4   5   6   7   8   9   10

For Rene

Contents

Preface

It happened a little over a year ago. I was riding my cycle—innocently enough but perhaps a bit too fast—on the scenic Mt. Vernon Trail, a smooth stretch of asphalt that winds like a graceful black snake along the Potomac River near Washington, D.C., rising over sun-lit ridges before ducking suddenly into dark woods and ravines. At the northern end of the trail I nodded a salute to the soldiers raising the flag on Iwo Jima and looked across the field of white crosses that dot the gentle slopes of Arlington National Cemetery like so many wildflowers. I couldn't help but think of the men and women in Afghanistan, Iraq, and other outposts, some of whom will one day make a last journey to this hallowed ground.

Peddling west along the Potomac, I took in the panorama of memorials, glistening in the morning sun—Lincoln, FDR, and Jefferson. In the far distance, beyond the Washington Monument, I caught a glimpse of the Capitol before taking a turn south toward the historic home of Martha and George Washington.

Approaching the steeper hills that guard the entrance to Mt. Vernon, I was clearly moving too fast on a sharp turn. In panic I hit the right brake. As the cycle came to an abrupt stop, I suddenly found myself taking a flying leap over the handlebars, coming face-to-face with the unforgiving asphalt. For a split second all my thoughts, patriotic and otherwise, vanished along with every sense of time and place. Emily Dickinson captured the experience when she wrote,

> Pain has an element of blank;
> It cannot recollect
> When it began, or if there were
> A day when it was not.

Other cyclists came to my rescue and, after a call on my cell phone, my wife, Rene, was on the scene to rush me to the emergency room. Despite my nightmares from watching *ER,* the personnel calmly attended to the wounds on my arms and legs, stitched up the deep gash in my upper lip, and attempted to push my teeth back into their appointed places. Then the doctors said, "Let's just take a CAT scan to be safe." Why not? In half an hour he returned, looked me straight in the eye and said, "There is a tumor on your brain." He added with more than a touch of irony, "You were very fortunate to have had this accident."

The short version of a long story is this: It is now more than a year later and I'm happy to report that the brain surgery was success-ful, the prognosis good, and I'm back again on my cycle, traveling—a bit more slowly, perhaps—the Mt. Vernon Trail. I recall this dramatic life incident because such moments—like death itself—have a way of focusing attention on the things that are important. Both before and after surgery, I thought a great deal about God, the meaning of life, and the love of family. I was filled with gratitude for prayers from friends, including those in the Jewish and Islamic communi-ties. Imagine being prayed for by Jews and Muslims!

I also thought a great deal about my country, the United States of America, and its role at this volatile moment in history. I recalled the exhilaration that accompanied the end of the Cold War in the early 1990s and the hope it created that enormous resources com-mitted to the East–West geopolitical confrontation might now be directed to the alleviation of hunger, disease, and oppression in the world. I recalled the terror attacks of 9/11, an event that appeared to shatter the dream. At the same time I asked myself whether this terrible moment in history might not—instead of shattering that dream—be a catalyst in its realization. Could not this occasion, I asked myself, inspire us as a nation, not only to launch a global war on terror, but a global war on poverty, hunger, and disease as well?

Instead, America has taken quite another course. This book raises critical questions about that course. It is not a protest of the war in Iraq, however, nor does it question the need for the creation of culturally appropriate democracies in the Middle East. But it does raise questions about the larger agenda of which the war in Iraq and the democratizing of the Middle East are elements. Although I will not hesitate to state my opinion on these issues, my primary purpose is to stimulate open, nonpartisan discussion of this critical issue, especially by people of the church.

Acknowledgments

I want to thank Rev. Conrad Braaten, senior pastor of the Church of the Reformation (ELCA) on Capitol Hill in Washington, D.C., for initiating this project and providing critical, supportive accompaniment throughout. I am grateful to Rev. John Moyer, recently retired director of the Geneva-based Frontier Internships in Mission (FIM). John has pushed the mission envelope by sending followers of Christ to build understanding and trust in situations "where angels fear to tread."

I am grateful for many friends who have read my manuscript and given counsel. The assistance of Brenda and John Peterson has been invaluable, as has been that of my colleague Phil Anderson, with whom I have worked closely on the peace processes in El Salvador and Guatemala. Thanks also to Carolyn and Fred Forsythe, Ralph Zorn, Stephen Larson, John Stumme, Anita Johnson, Ed Brown, colleagues in the Metropolitan Washington, D.C., Synod of the ELCA, among them Renate Eustis, Meredith Lovell, Jean and Dan Martinsen, Tom Knoll, and Mark Cooper, and family members Shelley and Steve Wee, Chris Wee, and David Wee. I am grateful to Ervin Rokke, president of Moravian College and Theological Seminary, and members of the Moravian community for their constant support. I want to thank Dr. Fred Gaiser, editor of *Word &*

World, for permission to quote from an article I had written in the Spring 2005 edition on "American Empire."

I am especially indebted to the Lutheran World Federation (LWF), a global communion of churches with whom I have been associated over a period of twenty-five years. The LWF is not only a channel for mutual support to its members as they carry out the church's mission; it is also able to express constructive critique of its members, as it did when it suspended two member churches during South Africa's anti-apartheid struggle.

The friends at Augsburg Fortress have been most helpful and supportive throughout, especially the editor of the Lutheran Voices series, Scott Tunseth, and his tough, but absolutely insightful copy editor, David Lott.

Above all I am grateful to Rene, who not only has a trained eye for anything that is out of touch with reality, but who has also accompanied this project with patience, love, and care from the day she rescued me along the Mt. Vernon Trail.

1

American Destiny: The Point of View

The view from Ground Zero

It was in the early 1990s, after the Berlin Wall fell and the era of the Cold War came to an abrupt end, that the church's long-standing vision of a new world order suddenly seemed possible. This vision of a more just and equitable global society was something the ecumenical churches had been talking and writing about for many years. With the end of the East–West geopolitical confrontation and the enormous resources that it demanded, they now asked whether this vision might now have a chance to become reality. The very thought of redirecting resources to alleviate hunger and disease was exhilarating. If ever there was a chance, it was now! If the dream were to be realized, it was also clear that a major role would fall to the one country people began calling "the one remaining superpower," the United States of America.

Yet it was on a cold day in January 2002 that this vision of a new world order became for me at once more distant, and yet more urgent, than ever. On that day I had the opportunity to stand on the wooden platform overlooking "Ground Zero," once home to the Twin Towers of the World Trade Center in New York City.

I recall the sun shining against a cloudless blue sky. There was an eerie silence on the platform as our group, all of whom had waited hours in a line that snaked its way through the streets of lower Manhattan, was ushered forward for its brief opportunity to look into the sprawling abyss of tangled metal and broken concrete. The only sound that could be heard was the groan of the tractors and trucks as they strained to pick and load the rubble. As we edged closer to the front of the platform several people began to weep. Some held tightly to relatives and friends. Some stared blankly into the abyss, thinking their own thoughts.

Peering into the still-smoldering crater where once stood the proud symbols of economic achievement, I felt a deep sense of sadness, as well as sympathy for the families of the nearly three thousand whose innocent lives were extinguished there so violently. Among the victims were people who had recently come to America from more than seventy-five countries.

Yet something else clearly was churning within me and within others as well. Call it reflection occasioned by a profound sense of vulnerability—the sudden realization that this platform was also a vantage point for looking into one's own soul and into the soul of America. The following is an attempt to take such a look, and to provide a vantage point for others to look as well.

Where are we going?

In spite of all that has happened since that day—increased polarization in the nation and the world, the expansion of Islamic extremism, acts of terror not only in the United States, but in Great Britain, Spain, Indonesia, Jordan, and other countries as well—I continue to believe that a new global order is possible. I also continue to believe that America has a major role to play to that end.

Yet as a Christian and as a U. S. citizen I have profound concerns about the future of this country and its role in the world. I know that I am not alone in this. Many people—people who attend church, raise the flag on national holidays, and watch the evening news—are increasingly asking: Where are we going as a nation? Are we pursuing a course that is consistent with our best traditions? What values do we as a nation have to share with the world community? And this question too: What does the church—and its message of hope in Jesus Christ—have to say at this volatile moment in history as our country seeks to redefine its identity and its mission?

Those who are leading our country also have a vision for a new world order. As President George W. Bush stated in his speech to the West Point graduation class in 2002, "America is a nation with a mission." What has become increasingly clear in the years since is that, in the face of setbacks in Iraq and growing criticism in the United States and abroad, this sense of mission remains very much in place. It is a mission to bring profound change to the political, economic, and cultural life of the world. I am not speaking here of an agenda that is either hidden or sinister. The policy that gives definition to this mission is official, well defined, and public, laid out for the world to see.[1] In January 2006 the President of the Council on Foreign Relations, Richard Haas, citing America's unprecedented military and economic strength, defended the basic contours of this mission, expressed in the thesis of his book, *The Opportunity: America's Moment to Alter History's Course.*

Although I have a number of questions for the prime movers who are driving this agenda (see chapter 3), I agree with them on two fundamental assumptions: (1) We are living at a unique moment in history, a time of immense opportunity to advance the cause of freedom, democracy, and respect for human rights throughout the world; and (2) in this new century the United States of America is called to assume a leadership role. What remains in question is how this opportunity will be used, what goals will be pursued, what means will be employed, and with whom the country will be willing to partner.

A genuine new world order is eminently achievable. Yet I believe that it has a chance to be realized only if our leaders make a number of fundamental changes in their stated agenda. In the following chapters I will discuss the shape that such an altered agenda will need to take. Can such a course correction take place? By all means! This nation is remarkably resilient. If people are willing to express themselves—and here I address the people of the church in particular—they will have helped to give new shape to the nation's role in the world. Such a new shape, I contend, will need to be in harmony with the nation's still-valid Puritan vision to be a light to the nations and a beacon of hope to the world.

This modest book is not a protest of either economic globalization, the war in Iraq, the U. S. role in the Palestinian-Israeli conflict, or the conduct of the war on terrorism. Rather, it addresses the larger agenda to reorder the world and the ethical and quasi-religious assumptions on which this agenda is built. It is intended to stimulate an urgently needed national debate based on open, nonpartisan discussion of America's new global agenda. As an impetus to a wider national debate, it encourages dialogue within our church's congregations, colleges, and seminaries and will suggest ways in which concerned church members might positively respond. I cannot claim to be without bias, of course. I do hope, however, that the following chapters will elicit discussion and response to an issue that is already having a profound effect on the lives of people everywhere.

The view from my ministry

These reflections on the future course of our country rest on three commitments shared with others who are part of the communion of the church: (1) our commitment to the *gospel* as the power of God's grace to renew all of human life, including the life of our nation; (2) our commitment to the *church* and its calling to proclaim the gospel of God's grace manifest in Christ, administer the sacraments, and to be both partner and constructive critic (sentinel) to the civil authorities who have been entrusted with the responsibility of ensuring peace and justice; and (3) our commitment to our *country*, the United States of America, and to finding ways to best pursue our calling as a nation among nations—set forth in our founding documents and traditions—to be a beacon of justice to all the world. Allow me to explain each of these commitments.

1. The gospel

The heart of the church's message is the announcement that God has acted in history through the life, death, and resurrection of Jesus Christ to bring redemption, renewal, and wholeness to the world. I state this at the outset, not only to make clear my own faith assumptions, but also because I believe that the power of this same gospel is able to bring healing and hope to the lives of both individuals and communities.

Commitment to Christ is very personal, of course, experienced in the discipline of daily prayer and meditation. Yet it also has a social dimension in that what the church calls the power of grace holds the key to transformation and healing in situations of alienation and conflict within and among communities. The examples of such transformation are legion. Having worked for more than twenty-five years both as a parish pastor and within the global, ecumenical ministry of the Lutheran church, I have been fortunate to experience the power of the "new creation" (Gal. 6:15) in ways that go beyond the usual individualistic interpretations of the gospel.

The dynamics of transformation through the gospel—including identification with human brokenness and the willingness to bear its pain through sacrificial love—were at the heart of efforts to overcome the terrible legacy of apartheid in South Africa. Some might recall the day when Anglican Archbishop Desmond Tutu, chairman of the South African government's Truth and Reconciliation Commission, announced amnesty to the four black men who had confessed to killing the young, white American Fulbright scholar Amy Biehl in 1993. It was a dramatic moment, filled with anger, grief, and regret, as the men made their public confession. When the word of forgiveness was spoken, it was as if a waterfall of emotion had been released. The scene of Amy's parents embracing the killers and weeping with them is indelibly etched in my memory, as are their words on that day: "Amy was drawn to South Africa as a student and she admired the vision of Nelson Mandela of a 'Rainbow Nation.' It is this vision of forgiveness and reconciliation that we have honored."[2]

I recall also the day when South African Reformed Church pastor Alan Boesak risked his own life as he made his way through an angry crowd to rescue a man who was deemed to be an informer, about to suffer death by "necklacing," in which a tire filled with flammable liquid was placed around the neck and ignited. This single act of selflessness tapped into that strange power of vulnerability and sacrifice that is manifest in Jesus Christ.

The power of the gospel to bring hope out of despair was never more vividly illustrated for me than on the day in 1979 when I encountered some three hundred students from the Manama Lutheran School who had been chased by soldiers of Rhodesia's white supremacy regime into the rugged bush of northern Botswana. Exhausted, bruised, and anxious about their future, their bishop, Jonas Shiri, asked them what they wanted most. Given the fact that they all faced the possibility of death—and that the soldiers would most likely kill some of them in the coming months—the response by a fourteen-year-old gave me a shock: "Bishop, we would like very much to finish our confirmation instruction." The child's request—and the bishop's prayer—was a moment that seemed to lift this bizarre jungle scene into the very presence of God. When someone asked if we could all sing a song together before we left, I simply lost my composure. Remembering the song from days of Sunday school, I attempted to join in: "God be with you till we meet again / Till we meet, till we meet, till we meet at Jesus' feet / God be with you till we meet again."

I relate these stories because they recall moments in which the power of what the church calls "the gospel" transformed the lives of both individuals and communities. We do not control or program this power, of course; it comes and goes like the wind. The day in 1989 the Berlin Wall came crashing down, the day in 1990 that Nelson Mandela walked freely among his people, the day in 538 B.C.E. that King Cyrus announced that the children of Israel could return to their land—all have this in common: They expressed the amazing, healing, liberating power of God in history. We can only prepare for its coming, point to its source, witness to its power, and celebrate it in drama and poetry, in dance and song. It is this same power that holds the key to overcoming the deep divisions that exist in the world community today.

2. The church

Second, this book is written out of a commitment to the "one, holy, catholic, and apostolic church" and to its visible expression in the life of the world. In essence, the church is the community that is "called out" of the world for worship, the preaching of the Word, and the celebration of the sacraments, and then sent back into the world to witness to the power of God's grace in work, family, and the community's social, economic, and political life. The call of each individual that makes up Christ's church is to serve God for the good of the neighbor, regardless of occupation, be it pastor, nurse, lawyer, farmer, housewife, computer programmer, salesperson, politician, soldier—all are called to serve God in their work.

Countless individuals and congregations in many lands have fulfilled this call in their own creative ways, and thereby pushed the envelope of conventional wisdom and the rules of the status quo to embody the essence of what it means to be the church, the Body of Christ in the world. Among a great number of individuals and congregations from our own country who have taken such courageous action, some names come immediately to mind:

Rev. Gustav Schultz, campus pastor in Berkeley, California, in the early 1980s took a lonely journey to the scattered Christian communities in the Democratic People's Republic of Korea. Although the U. S. government did not support this pioneering visit, it served to give important recognition to growing Christian congregations in North Korea and paved the way for visits by many others.

Dr. Edward May dedicated his ministry to the liberation of Namibia and South Africa from the oppressive system of legalized racism known as apartheid. He spoke the unvarnished truth at the United Nations and at government offices in Washington, D.C. His *Namibia Update* was regularly on the list of periodicals banned by the South African government, making him *persona non grata* in the countries whose people he supported in their liberation struggle.

Ruth Youngdahl Nelson, author, speaker, 1973 Mother of the Year, put her body on the line when she protested the production of nuclear weapons, chaining herself to the gate of a leading weapons manufacturing facility. With her son, Ruth rowed her boat in front of the Trident nuclear submarine in Puget Sound. With the Lutheran Peace Fellowship in 1983, she startled the Soviet Peace Council in Moscow by unfurling a packet of pictures of her grandchildren and pleading for an end to nuclear confrontation, prompting members of the Council to show pictures of their own families.

Rev. Roger Berg and his congregation, Newport Harbor Lutheran in California, defied convention—and more than a few rules—when they established a mechanism that made it possible for endangered families in Ethiopia to escape death during the Marxist government's campaign of detention and killing known as the Red Terror in 1978–79.

Rev. Jan Erickson-Pearson inspired Roman Catholic, Russian Orthodox, and Lutheran congregations to hold an ecumenical worship service in Vilnius, Lithuania, at the height of the Cold War. In the face of government attempts to divide the churches and play them off against each other, she helped forge a vibrant ecumenical ministry and demonstrated the creative and courageous leadership of women.

Rev. Philip Anderson accepted the reality of personal danger when he accompanied Salvadorean refugees home from Honduras and

Guatemalan refugees home from Mexico. Once he defused a tense and potentially volatile situation by engaging a heavily armed militia in the woods of El Salvador. Phil played a helpful role in the churches' efforts to achieve negotiated settlements to the long-standing internal armed conflicts in both El Salvador and Guatemala.

Dr. Carl Mau, General Secretary of the Lutheran World Federation, was persistent in negotiating one of the first official visits to Lutherans who had been forcibly scattered throughout Siberia and the Asian republics of the Soviet Union in the twentieth century. To everyone's amazement congregations had held together without pastors or church buildings through decades of persecution and physical hardship. Over a million of these Christians emerged like resilient wildflowers breaking though the long Siberian frost.

I need to remind myself of such people and congregations in those times I get down on the church for what I consider to be its silence in the face of injustice. As we all know, it is easy to be critical of the weaknesses of the institutional church in its finite form—particularly its policies, programs, and public pronouncements. Yet, I have enough faith in the church—and enough historical remembrance—to believe that its occasional folly will not get in the way of its authentic mission to be an agent of healing and reconciliation through the power of the Holy Spirit. Indeed, I thank God for the renewal of the church's life through the grace of God, expressed in the phrase that captures the ongoing Reformation, *"ecclesia reformata sed simper reformanda"*—the church reformed but always to be reformed. In light of this reforming grace and of its call from God, I believe at this present time in history it is crucial that the church—individuals, congregations, national church leaders—take courage from the witness of these and other saints of the ecumenical church to address America's efforts to bring about a new democratic order to the world community.

3. The country

Third, this study grows out of a commitment to the country of which I am a citizen, the United States of America. I am grateful for its heritage and the ways in which it has served as a beacon of hope for people around the world. Just as it has been entrusted with many gifts, it has also been called to awesome global responsibility in the twenty-first century.

In the course of my own ministry there have been many occasions in which a working relationship with units of the U. S. government has been very helpful. I think, for example, of the times the U. S. State Department assisted Lutheran Immigration and Refugee Service in the resettlement of political prisoners from Eastern Europe and granted visas to church leaders from communist lands to travel to this country. I recall the long history of government partnership that Lutheran World Relief has enjoyed in feeding the hungry, responding to disasters, and carrying out long-term, integrated development programs. I speak for many friends in the Baltic States of Estonia, Latvia, and Lithuania in expressing gratitude for the daily programs of hope beamed by Voice of America during the communist period. Even though I have been critical of some of our government's policies over the years, I have always felt gratitude for our nation's commitment to individual rights and freedoms.

It is in the deeper context of this fundamental appreciation and respect for our nation and its heritage that I call for this period of critical questioning and dialogue among the people of our church and between church people and leaders of government. The church needs to address a number of interrelated issues, among them, growing religious extremism at home and abroad, the harmful side of economic globalization, the export of American entertainment culture, and the increasing danger of natural disasters caused in part by global warming. At issue is not only the future course of American leadership in the world, but the quality of life on the planet itself.

None of us is without political bias, of course. But I hope that, out of a shared commitment to our country's role in the furthering of justice and peace in the world, people of every political persuasion in the congregations, synods, colleges, and seminaries of the church will join in serious reflection on the present course our country is taking. This includes not only reflection on the shape of the stated agenda for a new world order and the various policies that are in place to implement it, but also about the ethical and ideological assumptions that seek to justify that agenda.

The church's role as sentinel

One of the tasks of the church, as noted above, is to keep a watchful eye on those who govern. This calling has its roots in the tradition of the prophets and their protest against injustice in society. Recall for a moment the images of Jeremiah, Ezekiel, Amos, and Micah railing before the authorities on behalf of the poor. The image of Jesus on trial before leaders of the Roman Empire is one of the most powerful symbols of nonviolent resistance to political authority in all of human history.

While the primary function of the church is to proclaim the good news that we are redeemed from the powers of sin and death by grace alone, it also has the task of reminding the state of *its* obligations under God. This critical stance has long been at the heart of the church's ministry. For Christians of the evangelical tradition this critical stance is historically anchored in the Reformation's protest against the abuse of power by both church and state.

Martin Luther reminds us that the state does not constitute an independent and autonomous realm, subject to rules that have nothing to do with God's will.[3] Rather, the governing authorities function as God's instruments to ensure justice and peace and to guarantee the well-being of all the people. It remains the role of the church to maintain critical watch on the affairs of government—to be, as Martin Luther King Jr. once said, "the conscience of the state."

This study—and its invitation to open dialogue—falls into that critical tradition. It is written out of a commitment to the church's calling to be a "sentinel" or "watchperson," to keep a lookout on those who govern. It invokes the image of the ancient sentinel who had the responsibility of keeping vigil on the city wall, always alert for signs of danger.[4]

It is neither within the range of my competence—nor is it the purpose of this study—to deal with, for instance, the complex issues that belong to U. S. foreign policy or U. S. military strategic planning, though such issues obviously impinge on the agenda for a new world order. Rather, it is my intent to examine the contours of the overall agenda that the United States is now implementing as well as the ideological and quasi-religious assumptions upon which that agenda is built.

Terminology and overview

Let me say a word about the terminology I use in this book and provide a general outline of the chapters. First, I will use the term "America" synonymously with "the United States." I am reluctant to do this simply because there are a great many non-U. S. citizens who call themselves American. I bow to common usage, but with apologies to them.

The term "church" will most frequently refer to its institutional form, that is, the Roman Catholic, Orthodox, and Protestant bodies. Yet all of these institutional forms find their source and unity in the *ecclesia,* the universal church of Christ, the communion of saints. The term "ideology" will be used to refer to a system of ideas and beliefs that provide the basic justification for a social, economic, or political system. The term "quasi-religious" will refer to expressions such as *God, providence,* and *destiny,* that resemble religious concepts but are employed outside of a specifically religious context.

In the chapters that follow, I will first look at the concept of American Destiny, formulated by John Winthrop as "a city on a hill," that has given abiding shape to America's self-understanding through-out history. From there I will examine the ways in which political lead-ers today understand this sense of America's calling and raise critical questions about the values and ideology that are driving the global agenda to bring democracy and free-market capitalism to the world.

As an example of the dangers posed when a perverted vision of national destiny co-opts the church's proclamation, I will next exam-ine the early stages of the rise of National Socialism in Germany in the 1930s, with emphasis on the way in which people of the church were induced to support an ideology that claimed to be good for the nation and the world. I will claim that striking similarities exist between the German Christian movement then and the so-called Christian Right in America today.

My final chapter will ask how the church, based on its heritage in the Scripture and the Reformation, can bring its unique resources to bear on American's self-understanding and the shape of its mission to change the world. The epilogue will ask the question for our day that was asked by Dietrich Bonhoeffer in his "Who is Jesus Christ for us today?"

Questions for reflection and discussion

1. Did the events of 9/11 change your attitude about America and its role in the world? If so, how?

2. The author names some U. S. church leaders who have taken risks—and even defied political authority—for the sake of their ministry of peace and reconciliation. Can you name others?

3. Are you concerned about the present direction of our country? In what respects?

4. What do you understand to be the biblical rationale for the church's role as sentinel or watchperson over the affairs of government?

2

America's Calling: The Puritan Heritage

The indigenous/biblical vision

One of the most moving experiences of my life came during participation in the International Indigenous People's Summit, held in conjunction with the Earth Summit of 1992 in Rio de Janeiro, Brazil. From all over the world indigenous people gathered on a mountain not far from the sprawling city of tents that was part of the historic meeting of the U. N. Commission on Sustainable Development.

The week's agenda had to do with many concerns, such as the depletion of rain forests, indigenous rights and local law, government exploitation through tourism, access to clean water, cultural recognition, use of language, health care, and the like. But what I will remember most was the day that I was invited to share in a time of meditation with indigenous people on the mountain's highest plateau. We sat on the grass in front of a large, multicolored teepee as a bonfire crackled and drums beat out a steady cadence. The sound of a flute in the background seemed to blend with the slender, pink clouds and the warm evening breeze that wafted in from the Atlantic.

When I took a puff on the long pipe that was being passed around the circle and handed it to a man from Bali seated next to me, I was overcome with what I can only describe as a profound sense of oneness with people—and oneness with earth and sky and sea and air as well.

One might easily dismiss such a feeling as a romantic escape from the real world—or perhaps attribute it to the smoldering substance in the pipe! But I have a different explanation. There are moments in life in which we are allowed to catch a vision of the whole, when the primordial unity of creation is sensed, when we are given a glimpse into the mysterious bond between things and people, women and men, old and young, past, present, and future, my land and all lands. For me this was such a moment.

As those who have had similar experiences will testify, such moments, however fleeting, allow insight into the interrelatedness and interdependency of everything within the world. They are moments of transcendence, of holiness. The authenticity of this vision of unity is, of course, not established by empirical investigation or rational argument. It is simply given. Either you see it or you do not.

This sense of the unity and harmony of the creation is not unlike the biblical picture of God's creative sovereignty over all things as expressed in the early chapters of Genesis and celebrated in the Psalms. As indigenous people know well—and this includes the ancients of the Hebrew Bible—the creation is not a neutral "thing" to be analyzed and exploited; nor is the historical flow of temporal events a mere chronological record of things that happen. Nature and history, as we initially experience them—that is, *before* we begin to dissect and analyze—are, rather, dimensions of the primordial wholeness and harmony that unites all created things in what might be called a spiritual bond.

There were over a thousand different indigenous tribes on the North American continent before the Pilgrims even thought about setting sail. Their stories, myths, and legends, as well as the colorful rituals that give them expression, are extremely diverse. Yet a common thread unites many of them. In his book, *The Earth Shall Weep: A History of Native America,* historian James Wilson discusses this great diversity, and adds, "Yet for all their range and variety, these stories often have a similar feel to them. When you set them alongside the biblical Genesis, the common features suddenly appear in sharp relief; they seem to glow with the newness and immediacy of creation."[1]

What does this all-encompassing vision of a meaning-filled creation have to do with one nation's vision of its own role in the world? Based upon both of these biblical and primordial understandings, the answer is this: Every vision of a particular group, whether family or cult, tribe or nation, is measured by its ability to serve the larger vision of harmony and justice. In Scripture, justice does *not* mean "giving everyone their due," or conforming to a code of law. It means establishing the conditions of harmony or *shalom;* it means embracing nature and history, animals and trees and people; it means including the weak, the lame, the blind, accepting orphans and widows, welcoming the stranger, sharing the wealth of the earth with equity.

When the children of Israel limit their vision to what is self-serving—a golden calf, a mountain, a land, a city, a temple—the prophets come to remind them of the one God who is neither their own property nor the lord of their particular space. This tension between—on the one hand—loyalties to gods of particular nations, ideologies, places, and—on the other—loyalty to the one God of universal justice is expressed eloquently in Psalm 82 as Yahweh holds a great council and summons the gods of injustice to account:

God has taken his place in the divine council;
in the midst of the gods he holds judgment:
"How long will you judge unjustly
and show partiality to the wicked?

Give justice to the weak and the fatherless;
maintain the right of the afflicted and the destitute.
Rescue the weak and the needy;
deliver them from the hand of the wicked."

They have neither knowledge nor understanding,
they walk about in darkness;
all the foundations of the earth are shaken.

I say, "You are gods,
children of the Most High, all of you;
nevertheless, you shall die like mortals,
and fall like any prince."

Rise up, O God, judge the earth;
for all the nations belong to you!

From the standpoint of biblical faith, any discussion of a country's vision or sense of destiny needs to be measured by the larger vision of the essential unity, harmony, and integrity of the world that the one sovereign God created and sustains. It is to the recovery of this larger vision of justice *(shalom)* that the prophets called the people. It is to the fulfillment of God's purpose for the world *(kosmos),* not for a particular nation, that the disciples and apostles call all people—women and men, rich and poor, Greeks and Romans, Jews and Gentiles alike. It is for the sake of the redemption of all creation that Jesus lived, died, and rose again, as Paul writes in Colossians 1:15-20:

He [Christ] is the image of the invisible God, the firstborn of all creation; for in him all things in heaven and on earth were created, things visible and invisible, whether thrones or dominions or rulers or powers—all things have been created through him and for him. He himself is before all things, and in him all things hold together. He is the head of the body, the church; he is the beginning, the first-born from the dead, so that he might have first place in everything. For in him all the fullness of God was pleased to dwell, and through him God was pleased to reconcile to himself all things, whether on earth or in heaven, by making peace through the blood of his cross.

The puritan vision

It is against this background that we now turn to that vision which has played such an important role in shaping the American self-understanding. The phrase *American Destiny* has been used through the course of American history, but perhaps more frequently following the end of the Cold War in 1989, and especially following the terrorist attacks on the United States on September 11, 2001. As the word *destiny* itself implies (from the French *destinée*, which means "to determine"), it has been used to express the belief that America has been set on a predetermined course and called to fulfill a specific purpose or goal.

Does America have a vision, a destiny, an inner goal[2] that seeks historical fulfillment? The earliest settlers understood themselves as fulfilling a missionary calling to be a light of freedom and justice to the world. They felt themselves called by God to embark on an exodus from the bondage of oppression in Europe and to enter the promised land of freedom and opportunity. The Puritans understood themselves to be the new Israel, summoned by Providence to overcome the demons of the old world by creating something qualitatively new and good.[3]

John Winthrop, who became the first governor of Massachusetts, recorded what is perhaps the classic statement of American destiny as he sailed for America aboard the *Arabella* in 1630. In his sermon, "A Model of Christian Charity," Winthrop expressed his vision of God's divine purpose for the colonies:

> Now the only way to avoid this shipwreck and to provide for our posterity is to follow the counsel of Micah, to do justly, to love mercy, to walk humbly with our God, ... we shall find that the God of Israel is among us, when ten of us shall be able to resist a thousand of our enemies, when he shall make us a praise and glory, that men shall say of succeeding plantations: the Lord make it like that of New England: for we must consider that we shall be as a City upon a Hill ...[4]

It belonged to the calling, the vocation, of the new country that it work for justice in this new land and in all the world. In its earliest formulations this was by no means an arrogant creed of imperial design, but a call to responsibility toward humanity and accountability to God. In the portion of his speech that is rarely quoted, Winthrop continues,

> ... the eyes of all people are upon us, so that if we shall deal falsely with our God in this work we have undertaken and so cause him to withdraw his present help from us, we shall be made a story and a byword through the world, we shall open the mouths of enemies to speak evil of the ways of God; ... we shall shame the faces of many of God's worthy servants, and cause their prayers to be turned into curses upon us till we be consumed out of the good land whither we are going.[5]

He concludes, "Therefore let us choose life, that we, and our seed, may live; by obeying his voice, and cleaving to him, for he is our life, and our prosperity."[6]

This image of a people called to establish the New Israel in a land of promise has become an integral part of American self-understanding since the nation's earliest days. It became, in the words of sociologist Robert Bellah, part of "the American civil religion,"[7] a unique blend of the pioneer spirit and elements of the Judeo-Christian heritage. As biblical scholar Richard Horsley has noted in his excellent book *Jesus and Empire*, it was Thomas Jefferson, the acknowledged father of the "wall of separation" between church and state, who originally "proposed that the Great Seal of the United States display Moses leading the Israelites across the Red Sea."[8]

This vision of the young nation, called by God to establish a new community in a promised land of opportunity and committed to "do justice, love mercy, and walk humbly with God," was later enhanced by the belief of Jefferson and others that all people "are created equal and endowed by their Creator with certain inalienable rights." This commitment to egalitarian justice, however, was gradually preempted by an ideology based more on privilege than on equality, more on a sense of status for some than responsibility to all.

The making of an imperial vision

As anyone who does research in the National Museum of the American Indian in Washington, D.C., will quickly discover, some early Americans used the identification of America with ancient Canaan to express an arrogant sense of privilege, which provided the rationale for driving Native American people from their lands. They regarded the Natives simply as inferior "Canaanites" who could be justifiably deprived of land, water, and personal dignity in order to fulfill their larger vision of "manifest destiny." For some colonists arrogant presumptions to special wisdom and virtue accompanied this sense of superiority and privilege. This is the sense of destiny that would increasingly become integrated into the American consciousness.

This distorted form of Winthrop's vision was used to justify dominance over Africans who were brought to America as slaves. Over against the democratic principle that "all people are created equal," which would be adopted in the founding documents of the country, was a deeply seated belief that only a chosen few were called to be free.[9]

The Spanish-American War, the event that more than any other brought the United States dramatically onto the stage of world history as a global and imperial power, also demands mention. This brief confrontation with Spain led to American military supremacy in the Western Hemisphere and to the acquisition of Cuba, Guam, Wake Island, Puerto Rico, and the Philippines. President McKinley, wondering what to do with the islands of the Philippines, expressed the condescending spirit that pervaded both church and state at the time: "There was nothing left for us to do but to take them all, and to educate the Filipinos, and to uplift and civilize and Christianize them, and by God's grace to do the very best we could by them as our fellow men for whom Christ also died."[10]

With respect to U. S. policy toward Latin America, one need only recall that, based on Teddy Roosevelt's interpretation of the Monroe Doctrine, any Latin American country could be justifiably invaded by the United States if there was any evidence of "flagrant wrongdoing." There was, however, no independent arbiter to determine what that meant in any particular situation. Yet under this mandate the United States in fact invaded a number of countries, among them, Colombia, Panama, Honduras, Guatemala, the Dominican Republic, Cuba, Haiti, Nicaragua, and Mexico.

On behalf of the founders

Given this history of imperial dominance it is not surprising that some observers decry the founders of the American republic as a group of greedy capitalist entrepreneurs who were determined to enrich their own coffers at any cost. These people claim that the American experience, from the time of the early settlers to the present, can only be understood in terms of the aggressive drive of wealthy men to use every available form of exploitation to further enhance their personal fortunes.

To be sure, there are examples of individuals who were in fact driven primarily by a quest for personal gain—and who employed a contorted understanding of the Bible to justify it. Such behavior is hardly limited to the past! Historian Charles Beard, in his controversial but well-regarded study of early American political history, *An Economic Interpretation of the Constitution of the United States,* documents the economic and financial interests of the framers of the U. S. Constitution.[11] Most scholars accept the conclusion that the men who were influential in its drafting, among them Alexander Hamilton, James Madison, and George Mason, were not simply concerned with the advancement of democratic principles.

Yet such studies notwithstanding, I believe it is irresponsible to conclude that the founders of the American republic had little commitment to the equality of all people and minimal desire that the "inalienable rights" of "life, liberty, and the pursuit of happiness" be translated into the laws of the land. On the contrary, they maintained a deeply held commitment to upholding the rights of the individual through the rule of law. To affirm otherwise, I believe, is to fall into a simplistic and highly partisan understanding of history.

Therefore, I make the claim that the Puritan vision of America—that it be a "city on a hill," an example of justice to the nations—was and remains a valid expression of our national purpose. For Winthrop the nation's very reason for being can only be grasped in the larger context of God's purpose for all creation. His vision was of a nation not born to privilege but to responsibility, not given to self-interest but committed to the common good.

This vision of American destiny is valid insofar as it understands the national destiny in terms that commit the unique gifts of America to the well-being of all people. This means that the "national interest" is valid insofar as it serves the global interest and that America's mission is valid insofar as it employs the unique gifts of this country for the well-being of all countries.

Even in a day of immense danger, when the country's borders are not able to be as porous as they once were and we all must accept the inconveniences of "homeland security," this vision remains a watchword for America. Emma Lazarus's well-known poem about the Statue of Liberty, "The New Colossus," expresses this poignantly:

"Give me your tired, your poor,
Your huddled masses yearning to breathe free,
The wretched refuse of your teeming shore.
Send these, the homeless, tempest-tost to me.
I lift my lamp beside the golden door!"

The test of American destiny

Yet the critical question remains, a question about our actual conduct as a nation: Has the United States endeavored to fulfill its calling, to keep its promise? If one agrees with my assertion that Winthrop's classic statement of American destiny is valid in principle, can it also be said that it has been implemented? The real issue at stake is not whether the nation's calling is articulated in *words* that reflect values that are good and just, but whether the actual *behavior* of the nation conforms to these values. Therefore the question: Have these noble words been put into practice?

The millions who immigrated to America from many lands in order to find freedom and opportunity—my grandfather among them—would doubtless answer yes. Others, like many who survived the African slave trade only to find poverty, racism, and more slavery, might answer differently. As has been noted, Native Americans, Latin Americans, and others who have been the victims of policies resulting from the vision of manifest destiny might well feel that we are dealing here with a sharp contradiction between words and actions.

In his classic study *The Irony of American History,* theologian Reinhold Niebuhr addresses the tension between ideal and reality.[12] He claims that not only the former Soviet Union contradicted its idealistic sense of purpose by its actual actions in history, but America has as well. For Niebuhr, American history is ironic insofar as history itself has refuted the original vision of America as a beacon of freedom and justice to the nations. Pretensions to virtue and innocence, which are at the heart of the national faith in the ability to master history, have at times been contradicted by the nation's actions in history. Irony is present when there is a failure to realize the contradiction.

For Niebuhr the epitome of irony is captured in the figure of Don Quixote. Setting out with a noble Enlightenment vision to change the world for good, he fails to realize that reality contradicts his idealism. He does not comprehend that the formidable giants he sees are simply windmills, his shining armor is rusty, and his mighty stallion is just a nag. Likewise, the American faith in its own inherent goodness and its ability to overcome evil in history suffers the ironic contradiction of that faith by failing to perceive its own weakness and limitations.

The vision of global dominion is invariably couched in terms of altruism. Thus the British Empire of the nineteenth century, under Queen Victoria and Prime Minister Benjamin Disraeli, pursued a policy of subjugation and exploitation in India and Africa under the banner of bringing God, law, and morality to an uncivilized world. Thus National Socialism in the 1930s in Germany (see chapter 4) began with an appeal to restore national dignity and offered bread and work to those who had neither. Communism appealed to the masses alienated by the Industrial Revolution, offering them a vision of egalitarian justice. Only later, when it was too late, did people begin to realize that the very foundations of this grand vision contained tragic flaws. If history is our teacher, we need to look carefully at past examples of claims to global hegemony, the hopes they inspired, and the disasters they created.

Comparing America's mission to bring freedom and democracy to the world to the mission of the British Empire to bring civilization to Africa and India more than a century ago, South African Methodist Bishop Peter Storey, who was on the forefront of the anti-apartheid struggle, asks this:

> Could it be that there is a new arrogance abroad in today's America? The arrogance of Empire? It may be that those who lead this most powerful nation in the world are more sure than they should be that they can control even unintended outcomes. I was born into the last days of another Empire, one upon which, we were told, the sun would never set. As I look back upon that Empire, I recall how *sure* we were about how *good* we were, and how *right* we were. I know now often we were *bad* and *wrong*.[13]

If Christian faith offers us insight into this situation, it is in the realization that there might be a beam in our own eye that prevents us from seeing the speck in our neighbor's eye. Paul knew well that it is not only bad people with bad motives who do bad things. All too frequently "good" people—that is, people with motives designed not to harm but to help others—end up doing some very harmful things. Paul's letter to the church in Rome sums up this dilemma: "I do not understand my own actions. For I do not do what I want, but I do the very thing I hate. . . . I do not do the good I want, but the evil I do not want is what I do" (Rom. 7:15, 19).

It is this insight into the human condition that needs to be kept in mind when considering the merits of every nation's vision or purpose. This includes America's sense of its own calling, its own destiny. The critical issue is not simply how the national calling is formulated, but how it is *lived out* from day to day and from year to year.

In short, we need to remember two things: first, that a large gap remains between our national ideals and the actual realities of American life; and second, that any contemporary articulation of America's vocation deserving of our respect needs to be expressed in global terms—that is, in terms that recognize that the gifts of the nation are to serve the well-being of the global community. Should we fail in pursuing this goal, in Winthrop's words, "we shall be made a story and a byword throughout the world, we shall open the mouths of enemies to speak evil of the ways of God."

Questions for reflection and discussion

1. Have you ever had an experience of what might be called wholeness and the unity of creation? Please describe it. Why is it sometimes difficult to have such a vision?

2. What does it mean to say that a country has a destiny (or a purpose, a reason for being, a goal, a calling)? Does America need to have a sense of purpose? Why or why not?

3. In what ways has America's calling to be a beacon of hope been fulfilled? Where, if anywhere, do you feel that the nation has gone off course?

4. Do you believe that life has a purpose, an inner goal that strives for fulfillment? Does *your* life have such a purpose?

3

Pax Americana:
The Window of Opportunity

The great debate

It is time for a national debate to take place on the question of America's role in the world in the twenty-first century. Call it a debate about American destiny. What are the goals that we as a nation want to fulfill over the course of the next twenty-five, fifty, and one hundred years? What sort of nation do we want to become? What contribution do we wish to make to the human and natural environment of planet Earth? To be sure, debates are already taking place informally, in schools, churches, and in Internet chat rooms, but these discussions, valuable as they are, focus primarily on present military, political, and economic activity. Generally speaking, the discussion has thus far been piecemeal, focusing on Iraq, Afghanistan, Iran, the Israeli-Palestinian issue, the war on terrorism, and related issues.

What we need is a structured, nonpartisan debate, not only about the goals we wish to pursue as a national community, but about the ethical and ideological assumptions that can legitimately support such goals. Let there be no doubt that, in the absence of such a debate, our leaders will in fact put in place and implement an agenda of their own design. Indeed, this is precisely what is taking place today. America is moving forward to design and establish a new world order, a *Pax Americana* as some have called it, based on a blueprint for restructuring global relationships according to U. S. specifications. But little public debate on the long-term goals themselves or the means for accomplishing them has taken place. There is even less discussion of the ethical and ideological assumptions that are giving new and dramatic shape to America's role in the world. Because of its grass-roots nature—and its commitment to a perspective that purports to transcend partisan political controversy—what better place for such a debate to begin than in the church?

One remaining superpower

What are the contours of this new global agenda? There is no question that, at the dawn of a new century and millennium, the United States has emerged as the dominant political, economic, and military power in the world. But what are the responsibilities that go along with the status of being the "one remaining superpower"? Does the United States have a special responsibility to ensure world order? If the United States, in the words of former U. S. Secretary of State Madeleine Albright, is "the indispensable nation,"[1] what exactly does this mean? Indispensable *for whom* and *for what?*

Theologian and social ethicist Gary Dorrien has asked whether there is a unique leadership role that the country is called to assume by reason of its vast military and economic power. He states:

> The United States is the most awesome power that the world has ever seen. Its economy outproduces the next eleven nations combined, accounting for 31 percent of the world's output. It floods the world with its culture and technology. It spends more on defense than the next twenty nations combined. It employs five global military commands to police the world; it has 750 military bases in 130 countries, covering two-thirds of the world; it has formal military base rights in forty countries; each branch of the armed services has its own air force; the U. S. Special Forces conducts thousands of operations per year in nearly 170 countries; the U. S. Air Force operates on six continents; and the United States deploys carrier battleships in every ocean.[2]

With military garrisons on four continents and a stated commitment to ensure the flow of raw materials needed for strategic supremacy, the United States has a difficult time convincing other nations that, unlike the Roman and British Empires, it has no territorial ambitions. It is clear, however, that the American military is increasingly being *perceived*—certainly by commentators of the foreign press—to be enforcing an order of world trade and political authority designed primarily to serve the national interest of one nation, the United States.

This perception was expressed violently on September 11, 2001. The destruction of the World Trade Center was clearly designed as an attack on a major *symbol* of U. S. economic dominance. In addition to being calculated to exact a huge cost in lives and dollars, this act of terror belongs to what sociologist Mark Juergensmeyer terms "performance violence,"[3] a piece of theater perpetrated for the purpose of conveying a message in a dramatic way. He goes on to say that, in the war against terrorism in which we are presently engaged, we would be remiss if we did not consider seriously the resentment that has been created at the fact that it is primarily the United States that not only lays down the rules of trade, but benefits from them as well.

Whatever the critics might say, the stated goal of the United States is clear. As expressed in the National Security Strategy of the United States, ". . . the United States will use this moment of opportunity to extend the benefits of freedom across the globe. We will actively work to bring the hope of democracy, development, free markets, and free trade to every corner of the world."[4]

Moral supremacy and world order

Yet the rise of a revitalized sense of national destiny was evident before the terrorist attack on 9/11. Already in 1991, in the immediate aftermath of the collapse of the Soviet Union, a group of U. S. politicians and political theorists (sometimes called "neoconservatives") argued that a unique moment had now arrived in world history for the establishment of a new democratic world order. The disintegration of the communist empire, they argued, had created a window of opportunity for the creation of a new global order dominated by the only nation that was equipped morally, politically, and militarily for the task, the United States. Among this rising group, who argued effectively against a multilateral U. S. foreign policy, Charles Krauthammer of the *Washington Post* writes: "America's purpose should be to steer the world away from its coming multipolar future toward a qualitatively new outcome—a unipolar world."[5]

In his book, *First Universal Nation,* columnist Ben Wattenberg states that "a unipolar world is a good thing, if America is the uni." He makes a case for the unbridled assertion of American military, political, and economic superiority: "We are the first universal nation. 'First' as in the first one, 'first' as in 'number one.' And 'universal' within our borders and globally."[6] Author Joshua Muravchik, in his book *Exporting Democracy: Fulfilling America's Destiny,* writes similarly:

> For our nation, this is the opportunity of a lifetime. Our failure to exert every possible effort to secure [a new world order] would be unforgivable. If we succeed, we will have forged a *Pax Americana* unlike any previous peace, one of harmony, not of conquest. Then the twenty-first century will be the American century by virtue of the triumph of the humane idea born in the American experiment.[7]

Such ideas gained the power and advocacy they needed to flourish with the election of George W. Bush in 2000. A new cadre of policy makers called for a bold assertion of American power with less reliance on allies or on international mechanisms such as the United Nations. They were influential in the Administration's decision to withhold support for a number of multilateral international measures, among them the Kyoto Protocol to the United Nations Framework Convention on Climate Change (1997), the Anti-Ballistic Missile Treaty (1972), and the International Criminal Court (1998).

Yet it was on the fateful day of September 11, 2001, that their goal of American preeminence, based on unilateralism, unchallenged military supremacy, regime change, preemptive military action, and the establishment of a global, free-market economy, suddenly found the occasion and sense of urgency it needed. Not long after those terrorist attacks, the decision was made to respond to the Al Qaeda attacks on the United States by invading not only Afghanistan, but also Iraq. Yet in the larger strategy, the elimination of Saddam Hussein from Iraq was seen as only one step in the plan neoconservatives had been advocating for many years, namely the installation of pro-democratic, pro-American governments throughout the Middle East.[8]

My purpose here is not to introduce a debate on the pros and cons of the U. S. decision to invade Iraq or the manner in which intelligence was used to justify that decision. Rather, for the present discussion, I want to emphasize that the bottom line of the new global agenda, now termed "the Bush Doctrine," has been stated publicly and clearly: The present moment in history provides a window of opportunity for the United States to use its influence to replace a number of autocratic regimes with governments that are democratic and friendly to America. This policy, its advocates argue, is the only possible option that will avoid global chaos and prevent further attacks on the United States, and in fact belongs to what President Bush has referred to as America's "special calling." Speaking at the National Cathedral in Washington, D.C., a year following the terrorist attacks, President Bush painted the ultimate goal with a broad brush: "Our responsibility to history is clear, to answer these attacks and rid the world of evil."

In the minds of those who advocate a more assertive role for the United States in the post-Cold War, post-9/11 world, there can be no doubt this is America's moment for greatness. That God will bless these efforts is self-evident, a faith reflected in a great many public speeches by the President and his key advisors. It is perhaps summed up best in the quote (originally from Benjamin Franklin) inscribed on Vice President Richard Cheney's 2003 Christmas card: "If a sparrow cannot fall to the ground without His notice, is it possible that an empire can rise without His aid?"

The response of the church: Preliminary questions

Some have reasoned that the national interests of America are synonymous with the best interests of the international community and that the driving force of the American vision, based on a commitment to democracy and free-market capitalism, has always served the best interests of the planet. And indeed, in assessing this contemporary version of America's destiny, it must be said that, at least at first glance, it has compelling dimensions. Already Afghanistan has been delivered from the oppressive rule of the Taliban, Libya has been persuaded to give up its nuclear program, North Korea has promised to follow suit, the Syrians are out of Lebanon, and a parliament has been democratically elected in Iraq. Even if it exacts a high cost in American lives and the expenditure of billions more dollars, might it just be that the dividends will be overwhelming?

Imagine for a moment that autocratic governments in the Middle East, from Egypt to Saudi Arabia to Iran and Syria, suddenly become democratic. Imagine that hard-line Islamic clerics in Iran and Saudi Arabia are replaced with leaders committed to egalitarian democracy. Add to that a vision of peace, however that is to be attained, between Israelis and Palestinians. Assume, furthermore, that the United States is not looking to acquire territory or to occupy foreign lands. Just think of a global network of free markets and a steady, uninterrupted flow of oil both to boost the national economy and strengthen the country for its enlarged role in the world. In spite of unexpected difficulties in Iraq and a widening scope of terror by

Al-Qaeda and affiliated insurgent groups in many countries, one might say that we have the means to accomplish this. However you cut it, the vision of a new global democratic order under American leadership has a very definite allure.

It is perhaps safe to say that such a view might find a measure of strong support among many Christians in America, especially, but not exclusively, among the fundamentalists of the Christian right. I personally believe that any fair assessment of the administration's global agenda needs to discount the more extreme views of some of its most ardent religious supporters, for instance, Rev. Jerry Falwell, who claimed in January 2004 that "God is Pro-War" and Rev. Pat Robertson, who in 2005 publicly advocated that the United States undertake regime change in Venezuela by assassinating its democratically elected president, Hugo Chavez.

Nevertheless, this vision of a *Pax Americana* has not been received well in some quarters. The rising tide of anti-American sentiment, expressed in demonstrations not only in the Muslim world, but in some parts of Western Europe, Asia, Africa, and Latin America as well, is an indicator that the new global agenda will not be supported everywhere. Even in our own country a major divide exists over many of these issues, as illustrated in the closely contested presidential elections of 2000 and 2004, or in deeply split opinion polls about the war in Iraq. Yet what is at stake is the larger agenda of American hegemony, of which the Iraq war and other issues are but a part.

But how should the church respond to the emerging ideology of global preeminence and the shape that it is taking politically, economically, and militarily? Based on its biblical and confessional heritage, what does the church as *church* have to say about the new vision that is presently unfolding? And what does it have to say about the ethical and quasi-religious assumptions that are being called forth to justify this vision? If the church, following in the line of Jesus and the prophets, is called to be a sentinel, to warn of impending danger, what if anything should it be saying *now,* both to the politicians and also to the religious leaders who have given their blessing to the new American mission?

If there is no national debate—or discussion within the church— it will bring back difficult memories of the days leading up to the massive U. S. involvement in Vietnam. For its part the church cannot afford to default on the discussion of an issue that has such far-reaching implications for the life of the planet. I hope that the following questions, along with the brief responses, might encourage discussion of the church's participation in the great debate on the new shape of America's role in the world.

1. Should the church get involved in politics at all?

The Bible witnesses to the manner in which God's Word is brought to bear on the total life of creation, including the life of human beings in society. The church is "called out" to proclaim a message of hope through the power of grace as that is made known in Christ. Yet it is also called to be a channel for God's judgment on idolatry, social injustice, and oppression. Chapter 4 will deal with one historical example of what happens when the church denies its biblical roots and is silent in the face of gross injustice perpetrated by the authorities. As Dietrich Bonhoeffer reminds us, the church is called to live in the world *for others.* Involvement in the political process is not simply because politics is too important to be left to the politicians, but because the church proclaims Christ as Lord of life in all its dimensions. The question is not *if* the church should be involved in the political life, but *how.* This question will be addressed in chapter 5.

2. Does America really have moral superiority?

In spite of the multitude of speeches from political leaders and TV evangelists that assure us that we are the best and greatest and most benevolent of all peoples, the answer to this question is clearly *no*. Not only have "all sinned and fallen short of the glory of God"; history is replete with examples of how the United States has *not* always acted in the best interests of the nation or the world community. Beyond the witness of history, there is the profound biblical insight into the human condition. Not only do we do things intended to harm each other but, as Paul reminds us, the evil that we do not intend to do we end up doing anyway. To confirm the truth of these assertions one need only take an honest look into one's own heart and soul. We might well agree with the President of the Council on Foreign Relations that, "in history, no single country has ever possessed greater [military and economic] strength as the United States does today," but the question remains: Does this overwhelming military and economic preeminence translate into *moral* preeminence as well? As Americans we are naturally proud of our traditions and the values of equality, freedom, and opportunity that we proclaim. But the simple fact is that we have not lived up to these values. To claim that one has a special lock on virtue is simply part of the "haughty spirit [that] goes before a fall" (Prov. 16:18).

3. Are America's values universal?

When official U. S. policy speaks of the values of freedom, democracy, and free enterprise as being "right and true for every person, in every society,"[9] the church needs to take a giant step back. Just as "not every one who says 'Lord, Lord' is fit for the kingdom of God," so can it be said that everyone who speaks these cherished words—freedom and democracy for example—do not always mean the same thing. Anyone who is familiar with life in the German *Democratic* Republic (East Germany) during the communist period can testify to one gross misuse of that cherished word. Or consider the various meanings associated with the word *freedom*. Over the past decades, representatives of developing countries at the United Nations have complained that, in the North Atlantic region, the word *freedom* is invariably understood in individualistic terms (freedom of speech, religion, and so forth), while less attention has been given to the freedom of the *community*, including freedom for integrated community development and the freedom to have a guaranteed source of food. We love the ring of these great words—life, liberty, and the pursuit of happiness—but we need to gather with friends at home and abroad to ask what they actually mean in the context of the real world. Although we Americans enjoy a pluralistic society, it is also true that we can be insulated from the ways in which people from other cultures use language and how they view the world.

4. Why not seek to rid the world of evil?

The president's commitment "to rid the world of evil" was made in the context of the terror attacks of 9/11, an event that few would disagree represents something absolutely diabolical. The war on terrorism certainly demands the commitment of all people who value human life, including church people in this country and throughout the world. At the same time, the church is acutely aware of the fact that evil can also be found closer to home, that of *every person* it can be said that "out of the heart come evil thoughts" (Matt. 15:19). Martin Luther's phrase, *simil iustus et peccator* (at the same time justified and yet a sinner), means that even though a person has experienced forgiveness through God's grace, this person does not cease to do hurtful things. Every person has a potential for both good and evil. Just as there is some good in the worst of us, there is also evil in the best of us. On these biblical grounds it is extremely precarious to *identify* evil with an "empire" (Ronald Reagan's designation of the Soviet Union) or with an "axis" of countries (George W. Bush's designation of Iraq, Iran, and North Korea). As we are painfully aware, the church itself can do some very evil things. The church is called to acknowledge the demonic that lurks in its very own life *before* it talks about evil in the life of society. This confession is expressed in most churches every Sunday. To identify evil with some person or country *out there* not only makes it very difficult to perceive the evil in *one's own* heart; it also labels *them* as irredeemable, without value. Once such identification is made it becomes much easier to destroy them.

5. Is God on our side?

The church needs to answer this question in a straightforward, unambiguous way. The moment one claims that God is on one's side, the very sovereignty of the one God of justice is denied. History is replete with examples of what happens when God is enlisted to support a particular partisan position. British armies were assured of God's support as they went off to slaughter Indians fighting for their independence. The German soldiers in World Wars I and II wore belt buckles with the inscription "God with us" *(Gott mit uns).* U. S. soldiers sang "Praise the Lord and pass the ammunition" as they headed for France in World War I. President George H. W. Bush sought only to encourage the troops when he said, "[T]o every sailor, soldier, airman, and marine who is involved in this mission, let me say, you're doing God's work." Yet regardless of how virtuous the cause appears to us, equating it with God's cause is quite inappropriate—if not idolatrous. It is one thing for a chaplain to ask God's presence and protection for the men and women who go to war; it is quite another to presume that God is on the side of any one nation. As the psalmist confesses to God, "To thee belong *all* the nations" (Ps. 82:8). One task of the church today is to protest the numerous ways in which God is being co-opted by political and religious leaders to support a particular understanding of America's role in the world. Let God be God!

A question of perspective

The question before us is not only whether we have an adequate perspective on history, but whether we have a perspective on our own life and that of our nation. The question is whether we might be too close to ourselves, too quick to see the speck in our neighbor's eye, too gullible as we listen to a multitude of public statements assuring us of the goodness of our country's role in history. What is needed at this point, I suggest, is neither arrogant self-righteousness nor masochistic self-deprecation but candor.

Let it only be said at this point that the discussion of America's role in the world needs the perspective of friends from other cultures, other lands, and other faith traditions. Here the emerging dialogue between Jews, Christians, and Muslims can be extremely helpful. It needs the sensitivity of those in our midst who have lived and traveled abroad and the insight of people who are recent immigrants to our shores. What is needed is candor and conversation, the counsel of friends, and openness to the Holy Spirit.

Questions for reflection and discussion

1. When it is said that America is a nation with a "mission" and that it has a "special calling," how do you understand this?

2. Do you believe that America's dominant military and economic might gives it a special responsibility to provide global leadership in the twenty-first century?

3. Do you feel that America occupies a moral high ground above other nations? What are your reasons for your response?

4. Do you think it helpful to speak of a national goal "to rid the world of evil"? From a Christian perspective, what is right/wrong with this?

4

The Church Struggle: A Lesson from History

The perennial heresy: Silence

If there is any actual example from history that demonstrates what can happen when the church abdicates its role as sentinel, that example comes from the chapter of the church's life played out during the 1930s and 1940s in Germany. This example, about which a great deal has been written,[1] provides abundant evidence of what can result when church people are silent in the face of injustice. In this case we are speaking of the massive violation of the human rights of Jews, homosexuals, gypsies, the disabled, foreigners, and Germans who sought to correct the state's course. It gives agonizingly painful evidence of what can happen when Christian people conclude that the church has no business addressing the issues affecting the political life of the nation.

Unfortunately, even after the many decades that have elapsed since the deafening silence of the Evangelical and Roman Catholic churches in the face of the Holocaust, the genocide that claimed the lives of six million Jews, one continues to hear Christian people say that the church should be silent, that it should not get involved in the issues that affect the life of the community. The question (to which we shall return in chapter 5), of course, is not *whether* the church should be involved in the political life of the nation, but *how* it should be involved.

Learning from history

Before looking at the historical example, it needs to be stated clearly that I am *not* making a simplistic comparison between America in the first decade of the twenty-first century and Germany in the 1930s. The dissimilarities are readily apparent. The United States is a democratic and pluralistic society. Decision-making powers are vested in the people and their freely elected representatives. Our economy is based on free enterprise, allowing creative, hard-working individuals—both immigrants and native-born—to succeed.

To be sure, this is not the *only* story, as noted in chapter 2. Native Americans were deceived, driven from their lands, and denied basic rights. African Americans were abducted from their homes, shipped as cargo to the new world, sold into slavery, beaten, and lynched. They were subjected to racial discrimination that persists in some quarters to this day. Other groups carried deeply rooted ethnic and religious prejudices into the new land.

At the same time we also need to tell the powerful story of millions of immigrants who found new life and hope in America, from African Americans to the Scandinavian, British, Italian, Irish, and German immigrants of another era to the enterprising Vietnamese, Hmong, Cambodians, and Central Americans of recent decades. Ethiopians and Nigerians, Mexicans, Salvadorans, and Guatemalans, to name but a few, tell stories of freedom from economic hardship and political oppression. Such scenarios of exodus and new beginnings, of release from political, economic, and religious bondage, and the discovery of the rare gift of opportunity capture a major motif of American history.

Over against this picture of America, the Germany of the late 1920s and early 1930s was anything but a land of opportunity for all. Emerging slowly from the Depression and still burdened by the debilitating sense of failure and ostracism created by the Treaty of Versailles (1919), the country was ripe for something that would restore a sense of national identity and pride. When the new order finally did arrive, however, it was built on the sands of arrogant nationalism, racism, and a vision of national destiny designed to expand territory and subjugate conquered peoples. In such respects there is little parallel with the United States today. Between America now and Germany then there is, it would seem, only a stark contrast—a contrast between good and evil, opportunity and bondage, freedom and despotism.

Yet this does not mean that there are not lessons to be learned. Indeed, the period of the Third Reich holds a multitude of lessons for every generation, among them the dangers of isolationism, the abuse of power, the destructive nature of racism, as well as the virtues of preparedness, the need to forge genuine multilateral partnerships and establish international mechanisms for the defense of human rights. This chapter will concentrate on one lesson that has come to us because of the apostasy of the church. It graphically illustrates what happens when the church allows its message to be co-opted and corrupted by an alien ideology, in Germany's case the ideology of National Socialism. In particular it will ask if there is a parallel between the German Christian movement during the Third Reich and what in this country has come to be known as the Christian Right. In both cases, I will contend, we are dealing with aberrations of the gospel that have profound influence on the direction of the country.

One of the primary resources for this inquiry can be found in the life and witness of Lutheran pastor Dietrich Bonhoeffer, whose activity on behalf of Jews and his role in the resistance to the Nazi state cost him his life. President George W. Bush remembered Bonhoeffer gratefully in his speech to the German Bundestag in Berlin in 2002:

One of the greatest Germans of the twentieth century was Pastor Dietrich Bonhoeffer, who left the security of America to stand against Nazi rule. In a dark hour, he gave witness to the Gospel of life, and paid the cost of his discipleship, being put to death before his camp was liberated. "I believe," said Bonhoeffer, "that God can and wants to create good out of everything, even evil."[2]

Beyond his role in the Nazi resistance and his tragic death, Bonhoeffer deserves particular attention for his opposition to the teachings and practices of a large segment of the church that sought to fuse the gospel of Christ with the emerging ideology of National Socialism. This latter conflict, waged not against the government as such but against the majority within the church that had sold its gospel birthright for the porridge of an alien ideology, came to be known as the Church Struggle *(Kirchenkampf).*

The rise of the German Christian movement

Even before the 1930s in Germany a group of mainly Protestant Christians, clergy and lay, began to see the rise of National Socialism (Nazism) as the only viable path to recovering German national identity and pride following the humiliating defeat in WWI and the debilitating conditions imposed by Versailles. Equally as important, they viewed the Nazi movement as holding the key to a national *spiritual* awakening as well. The church, they felt, was called to be the guarantor of the nation's spiritual center, the heart and soul of the cultural life of the people. This calling could be fulfilled, they argued, only if the church's teachings and practice were adapted to the emerging ideology of the state.

These Christians formed the nucleus of what came to be known as the German Christian movement. The German Christians saw themselves as "storm troopers for Christ," with a mission to purge the church of Jewish influence and to restore its proper role as the bearer of national identity and culture. This meant, among other things, that the church itself had to become "racially pure" and totally committed to the emerging vision of the nation's destiny.

Although never overtly supported by some of the Nazi elite, Hitler publicly endorsed the German Christian movement during a special radio address in July 1933, after which the movement grew rapidly in popularity and influence. Its membership quickly reached six hundred thousand and its adherents assumed major positions throughout the administration of the Protestant church and in virtually all of the universities and theological seminaries.

Throughout the 1930s until the end of the war in 1945 the German Christians organized rallies, held marches, published books and tracts, and worked tirelessly to gain control of church facilities. When the movement managed to gain access to the German church tax system as well, its financial security was assured. The German Christians wrote hymns of praise to Hitler and Jesus and developed a theology that rejected the church's Judaic heritage while affirming the Nazi belief in Aryan supremacy and German ethnic purity. Soon the Nazi flag, the swastika, would be hanging in the churches and draped over the altar. Babies would be baptized into a community of loyalty to Hitler. Members of Hitler's paramilitary militia, the SA *(Sturmabteilung),* were encouraged to hold their weddings in the church, much to the admiration of the youth. For the German Christians the true church was no longer the universal priesthood of all believers, as Luther had taught, but rather those who were united by blood and race.

The German Christians also sought to justify their racist and nationalistic views by an appeal to the classic teachings of the Reformation, with many of their theologians twisting the historical theology of the church to accommodate Nazi ideology.[3] One of them, Paul Althaus, on Adolf Hitler's accession to power, wrote, "Our Protestant churches have greeted the turning point of 1933 as a gift and miracle of God."[4] Regarding the Nazi vision itself, he wrote, "We Christians know ourselves bound by God's will to the promotion of National Socialism, so that all members and ranks of the *Volk* will be ready for service and sacrifice to one another."[5] When in 1933 the church adopted the so-called "Aryan Paragraph," which excluded all non-Aryans from clergy rosters and church offices (mirroring the state's exclusion of non-Aryans from civil service positions), Althaus said that "the church must therefore demand of its Jewish Christians that they hold themselves back from official positions."[6]

Another leading theologian, Emanuel Hirsch, called the rise of Hitler "a sunrise of divine goodness after endless dark years of wrath and misery."[7] Hirsch sought to use scholarship in an attempt to separate Christianity from its Judaic origins. Similarly, Gerhard Kittel, known to pastors and scholars in many countries for his *Theological Dictionary of the New Testament,* also used his scholarship in an attempt to justify the worldview of National Socialism. In the face of growing critique of his efforts, he responded, "We must not allow ourselves to be crippled because the whole world screams at us of barbarism and a reversion to the past. . . . How the German *Volk* regulates its own cultural affairs does not concern anyone else in the world."[8]

Although some scholars, such as Rudolf Bultmann at Marburg, opposed them publicly, these pro-Nazi theologians maintained their place at the center of the church's life. They taught and preached, attended worship, and offered prayers. A generation of pastors, educators, and church leaders in the German Christian movement fell under their influence. Among the pastors and lay leaders who opposed their views, few dared to speak out for fear of being labeled un-Christian and unpatriotic.

The Confessing Church and the Barmen Declaration

It was in opposition to the German Christian movement and its blend of anti-Semitism, nationalism, and sense of imperial destiny that the Confessing Church *(Bekennende Kirche)* was born. It came into being, not as a movement of resistance to the state, but as a movement of opposition to the German Christians' attempt to dominate and Nazify the life of the German church. Dietrich Bonhoeffer was but one of several of its leaders. Reverend William Niemoeller, who had expressed a great deal of sympathy with the German Christian movement in earlier days, moved over to the Confessing Church in the summer of 1933 when it became clear that the Nazis were determined to implement their anti-Semitic policies. His brother, Martin Niemoeller, would become one of the leading figures in the Confessing Church, along with Swiss Reformed theologian Karl Barth, who was to provide the biblical-theological foundation for a movement designed to counter the German Christians' influence.

The formulation Barth chose was deeply rooted in Christian tradition. In its simplest form it was summarized in the earliest confession of the church, Jesus Christ is Lord. Few times in history has this proclamation had such a powerful effect than in Germany in 1934. Aware of the crisis in the understanding of national destiny that was sweeping the country and infecting the churches, 139 representatives from Lutheran, Reformed, and Union[9] congregations debated and finally adopted a number of statements that Barth had drafted. These brief articles of faith, which came to be known collectively as the Barmen Declaration, were not ostensibly political. But they had implications for the political life of the country at a time when the country was moving toward an almost messianic sense of its national destiny. Article 1 stated simply:

> Jesus Christ, as attested by Holy Scripture, is the one Word of God which we have to hear and which we have to trust and obey in life and in death. We reject the false doctrine that the Church could and should recognize as a source of its proclamation, beyond and beside this one Word of God, other events, powers, historic figures and truths as God's revelation.[10]

It was immediately apparent that this article ran directly counter to the position of the German Christians and their ideology, which understood Hitler to be nothing less than "God's revelation." Like the early Christians who took a considerable risk in proclaiming Christ (not Caesar) as Lord *(kurios),* the Confessing Church knew just how dangerous it would be to subscribe to Article 1 of the Barmen Declaration. It soon became clear that those who gathered in Barmen were testifying to the double-edged message of the gospel, namely, its affirmation of the sovereignty of the one God revealed in Christ, and, at the same time, its rejection of the false gods of blood and soil, race and nation.

Article 5 of Barmen spoke directly to the policy of the state that was designed to co-opt other areas of society, including the church, under both the ideology and organization of National Socialism, stating:

> Scripture tells us that in the as yet unredeemed world in which the church also exists, the state has by divine appointment the task of providing for justice and peace. We reject the false doctrine that the state should become the single and totalitarian order of human life, thus fulfilling the church's vocation as well.[11]

This article employed the Lutheran understanding of the two kingdoms to oppose Hitler's policy of *Gleichschaltung,* or synchronization, in which all areas of society moved in lockstep with the controlling mechanism of the state. As happened under communism and other autocratic forms of government, this policy called for accommodation by the church and other institutions of society.

Confession to resistance

Not all of the pastors and lay leaders who gravitated to the Confessing Church were willing to take the next step and become part of the active resistance to the state. In fact, many were conservative Lutherans who held to a distorted view of Luther's teaching on "the two kingdoms." They claimed that the state, the kingdom on the left, was completely separate, autonomous, and unrelated to the church, the kingdom on the right. As a result of this radical separation of the realm of the state from the realm of the church—an idea that has no basis in Luther's writings—many in the Confessing Church limited their protest to internal church issues. Few were willing to protest actions of the state or to take Bonhoeffer's counsel that Christians share in the suffering of the Jews by taking direct action to protest their persecution.

Yet a number of leaders of the Confessing Church, including the pastors who were part of its illegal seminary in Finkenwalde, understood there to be an organic connection between confessing one's faith and taking action in opposition to the government. As Bonhoeffer's friend and biographer, Eberhard Bethge, speaking of those within the group, said, "We became involved in resistance almost without knowing it. Most of us were unprepared for the consequences. We soon realized that there can be no confession without resistance, that we would soon have to draw the consequences from our statement of faith."[12]

But this was not the attitude of the many pastors in the Confessing Church. When it was demanded in 1938 that all pastors take an "oath of allegiance" to Hitler, pastors belonging to the German Christians readily complied. But many pastors in the Confessing Church decided to accept it as an obligation as well. It read,

I swear that I will be faithful and obedient to Adolf Hitler, the Führer of the German Reich and people, that I will conscientiously observe the laws and carry out the duties of my office, so help me God.

When the Synod of the Confessing Church gave its approval for the pastors to take the oath, Bonhoeffer was furious. This was, he reasoned, a direct contradiction of one's ordination vow. The issue of the oath led to a growing split between Bonhoeffer and the Confessing

Church. Following the "Night of Crystal" *(Kristallnacht)* in 1938 and its acts of terror against the Jewish population, Bonhoeffer lamented in a meditation on Psalm 74, that "while they burned all the meeting places of God in the land" (v. 8), there were no longer any prophets to cry out. While acknowledging that he himself, in the face of growing anti-Jewish actions by the state, was "guilty of cowardly silence when I ought to have spoken,"[13] Bonhoeffer saved his harshest accusations for his own church:

> The church confesses that she has witnessed the lawless applica-
> tion of brutal force, the physical and spiritual suffering of countless
> innocent people, oppression, hatred and murder, and that she has
> not raised her voice on behalf of the victims and has not found
> ways to hasten to their aid. She is guilty of the deaths of the weak-
> est and defenseless brothers of Jesus Christ.[14]

The church struggle then and now

Having surveyed some of the features of one of the darkest periods in modern history, we turn to the question of whether—in spite of many obvious differences between Germany of the 1930s and America today—there might also be some lessons to be learned. What might the Church Struggle that took place more than seventy-five years ago have to say to the church in the United States today? In 2006, the centennial of the birth of Dietrich Bonhoeffer, many congregations and institutions of the church took a closer look at his life and witness with a single question in mind: What does the Bonhoeffer legacy of confession and resistance have to teach us today?

Are we witnessing a dangerous blend of Christian faith and national-ist ideology in America today?

In recent years a number of church bodies have been taking a closer look at public statements of the Confessing Church, in particular the Barmen Declaration, for inspiration and guidance as they have sought to articulate a response to the challenges of post-9/11 America. In 2004, on the seventieth anniversary of the signing of the Barmen Declaration, a reform movement, "Confessing Christ" within the United Church of Christ in the United States wrote to all UCC leaders calling on them to remember the lessons of the Church Struggle by opposing the dangerous mixture of faith and nationalism in America today:

> The Barmen Declaration of the Confessing Church in Nazi Germany says that we listen to "the one Word, Jesus Christ, as attested by Scripture . . ." Confronting the 'German Christians' and their fusion of blood and soil with the 'one Word of God,' Barmen spoke a bold 'No'! . . . Today, we have to do the same with 'American Christians' who cannot separate nation from gospel.[15]

In his article, "An Elephant in the Sanctuary: Engaging Issues of War and Peace," Rev. Conrad Braaten, senior pastor of the Church of the Reformation (ELCA) in Washington, D.C., writes about the "subtle, yet powerful influence" of civil religion in the United States today.[16] According to Braaten, it is civil religion that is the elephant in the sanctuary, "the identification of faith with the prevailing national ideology." He goes on to say that civil religion is not to be confused with "healthy patriotism," namely, a commitment to "our nation's core values, that 'all people are created equal with certain inalienable rights and that among these are life, liberty and the pursuit of happiness.'" Rather, civil religion is present when "a sacred aura is conveyed to the existence of a nation-state, assigning to it a divine origin, a sense of divine guidance and a promise of divine destiny." In light of all this, Braaten asks, What does it mean to follow Christ at such a time? He answers with reference to Dietrich Bonhoeffer: "Bonhoeffer was convinced that the answer to this question was to be found in the study of the Scripture, in prayer and in theological discussion of the meaning of discipleship *within the congregation*" (emphasis his).[17]

Like many in the Germany of his day, however, Dietrich Bonhoeffer was himself caught up in a popular movement that, it was hoped, would restore dignity and pride to the German people and bring peace to Europe. In retrospect, however, Bonhoeffer felt that he had been blind to the hidden dangers, to the subtle ways in which national self-confidence and sense of purpose could turn into *hubris*. The problem, Bonhoeffer maintained, lay in the nation's arrogance, "in her belief in her almightiness, in the lack of humility and faith in God and the fear of God. . . . When the war broke out the German people did not consider very much the question of guilt. We thought it to be our duty to stand for our country and we believed of course in our essential guiltlessness."[18]

Although a comparison between the German Christian movement of the 1930s and 1940s in Germany to elements of the so-called Christian Right in America today might appear misplaced at first glance, we do well to remember Bonhoeffer's observation that such movements invariably grow out of idealistic visions that appear initially to embody so much good. The devil lurks in the subtleties, however, and in the failure of good people to discern pretense and arrogance in their own understanding of themselves and their world.

Has an "alien gospel" of law replaced the gospel of grace in Jesus Christ?

The most striking parallel between Germany of the 1930s and 1940s and America today, according to writer Donna Glee Williams, is that between the German Christian movement and elements of the Christian Right.[19] Although there are major differences between them, they have this in common: In both cases we are dealing with the co-opting and corrupting of the church's central proclamation by an alien ideology.

Just as the German Christian movement introduced an ideology based on an understanding of historical destiny rooted in God's providential law, the Christian Right in the United States is advocating its own cosmic worldview in our day. It is known by many names, one of which is dispensationalism. The particular form of dispensationalism that prevails among the Christian Right today, had its origins in the thought of British evangelist John Nelson Darby, who claimed that Scripture shows that God has a master plan for history, played out against an apocalyptic battle between good and evil, which will culminate in the great battle of Armageddon, followed by Jesus' establishing his thousand-year (millennial) kingdom in Jerusalem.

Not many years ago this fundamentalist theology of what has become the Christian Right could be relegated to the fringe of both church and society. But in recent years it has moved dramatically to center stage. The overwhelming popularity in the 1970s of Hal Lindsey's *The Late Great Planet Earth,* with its predictions of events during the Cold War, and more recently the best-selling *Left Behind* series by Tim LaHaye and Jerry B. Jenkins, give evidence of this. Based on opinion polls it is clear that millions of Americans subscribe to a dispensationalist view of history and believe that contemporary events are literal fulfillments of biblical prophecy.

Describing these views of the Christian Right, TV journalist and evangelical Christian Bill Moyers writes:

> Once Israel has occupied the rest of its "biblical lands," legions of the Antichrist will attack it, triggering a final showdown in the valley of Armageddon. As the Jews who have not been converted are burned, the messiah will return for the rapture. True believers will be lifted out of their clothes and transported to heaven, where, seated next to the right hand of God, they will watch their political and religious opponents suffer plagues of boils, sores, locusts, and frogs during the several years of tribulation that follow.[20]

Of the people who espouse these views, he notes, "[T]hey are sincere, serious, and polite as they tell you they feel called to help bring the rapture on as fulfillment of biblical prophecy. That's why they have declared solidarity with Israel and the Jewish settlements and backed up their support with money and volunteers. It's why the invasion of Iraq was for them a warm-up act, predicted in the Book of Revelation."[21]

Is the Christian Right helping to drive the new foreign-policy agenda?

The phenomenon of the Christian Right might be dismissed out of hand as innocuous and unbiblical were it not for two things: First, an increasing number of Americans—perhaps 40 percent according to some analyses—hold to dispensationalist views. Second, those who support such views occupy an increasingly large number of positions in the U. S. Congress and in the Administration. According to Moyers, nearly 50 percent of the 108th Congress (2003–2004) subscribed to these views and were backed politically by the increasing power of right-wing Christian organizations.[22]

Space does not permit a detailed description of the ways in which this apocalyptic worldview of the dispensationalists has been expressed by political leaders, especially by presidents Ronald Reagan and George W. Bush and members of the U. S. Congress, but mention needs to be made of the profound impact this ideology is having on the Palestinian-Israeli issue. Among fundamentalist dispensationalists, the "Christian Zionists," who have approximately twenty million adherents in the United States, have set an agenda for the Middle East that biblical scholar Barbara Rossing rightly calls "distorted and dangerous . . . a hazard to peace."[23]

This type of Christian Zionism, Rossing is quick to point out, has little to do with traditional Zionism, which is the movement of Jews to find a secure homeland in Israel, a goal supported in principle by the mainline churches. Rather, based on a gross misinterpretation of the books of Daniel and Revelation in particular, the Christian Zionists promote a militant scenario of Israel's conquest of the entire ancient biblical land, the expulsion of the Palestinians (including the Arab Palestinian Christians) who have lived on the land for millennia, the rebuilding of the Temple on the present site of the Dome of the Rock (the second-holiest site in Islam), and a campaign designed to prevent any peace agreement that would allow Jewish and Palestinian states to exist side by side. Prophecy allows no compromise. Given the fact that there is such strong support of these views among U. S. congressional members, it is not surprising that finding a fair settlement of the lingering Palestinian-Israeli issue is so difficult.

Many of the groups who are advocating a more strident use of American force today undoubtedly have little or no connection with dispensationalist groups. Yet whether or not these groups are religiously motivated, their agendas converge when it comes to U. S. policy in the Middle East.

The ideology of dispensationalism, then, like that of the German Christian movement, serves a very specific political agenda. Those who advance these views welcome the emerging view of American destiny, the war in Iraq, confrontation with Islam and the support of Israel's claim to the entire land of Palestine as part of God's plan for the salvation of the world. As Bill Moyers wrote in 2005, "I am not suggesting that fundamentalists are running the government, but they constitute a significant force in the coalition that now holds a monopoly of power in Washington."[24]

Although there are other factors that have contributed to the cultural divide in America today, one of them is certainly the influence of both the theology and partisan political activism of the Christian Right. It has undermined the vision of the common good and been detrimental to a fair settlement of the Palestinian-Israeli issue. This theology represents not only an aberration of the gospel of Christ; it is providing the theological underpinning for a vision of American destiny that is playing an increasingly influential role among national decision-makers. Like the German Christian movement in the 1930s and 1940s in Germany, this theology is dangerous for the country and the world.

Is the specter of anti-Islam and anti-Semitism looming in this ideology?

It is most troubling that some leaders of the Christian Right have expressed their dislike of Islam with such vehemence. Evangelist Franklin Graham is convinced that "the God of Islam is not the same God" as the God of the Christians, and that Islam itself is "a very evil and wicked religion." In media reports TV preacher Pat Robertson claims that Muslims "want to destroy Jews," and Jerry Falwell called the prophet Mohammed "a terrorist" on an episode of the TV newsmagazine *60 Minutes*.[25] Such remarks emerge from ignorance and bigotry and do not, I am confident, represent the attitudes of most Christians in America. Nevertheless, such erroneous views have fueled anti-Christian and anti-American feelings in many countries of the world.

But are we dealing here with a resurgence of anti-Semitism as well? On the surface, of course, the dispensationalists appear to be anything but anti-Semitic. After all, as we hear daily from the fundamentalist TV evangelists and many members of the U. S. Congress, God promised the entire land to Israel. The rebirth of the state of Israel in 1948 was part of God's plan, as will be the rebuilding of the Temple. The return of the Gaza Strip to Palestinian control in 2005 was troubling, but they insist that the prophecy is intact: The Jews must control all of Israel before Christ returns. That continues to sound very much like a pro-Jewish scenario!

To be sure, some Israeli leaders welcome the financial and political support from the Christian dispensational fundamentalists. They provide encouragement and support to the work of the so-called Christian Embassy in Jerusalem, an institution that actively propagates these ostensibly pro-Israel dispensationalist views. These leaders provide logistical and other types of support for the multitudes of Israel tours carried out by dispensationalist Christians from America. Such support, however, is primarily pragmatic, geared more to immediate needs than long-term goals.

Consider the "long-term" scenario of the Christian Zionists themselves—quite simply, it is that all Jews who do not convert to Christ will be incinerated. Bill Moyers notes, "As the Jews who have not been converted are burned the Messiah will return for the Rapture."[26] Barbara Rossing quotes Gershom Gorenberg, an Israeli Jew, who cited the danger of anti-Semitism in the dispensationalist worldview, during a *60 Minutes* telecast:

> They don't love real Jewish people. They love us as characters in their story, in their play, and that's not who we are. . . . If you listen to the drama they are describing, essentially, it's a five-act play in which the Jews disappear in the fourth act. . . . People who see Israel through the lens of Endtimes prophecy are questionable allies.[27]

A final question

In concluding this chapter I come back to the question raised at the outset: Can the church afford to be silent? It is, of course, relatively easy to look back on history and pass judgment on those times when the church missed an opportunity to speak and act. It is easy to talk about the apostasy of the church during the Third Reich. But what about the church in our own day? The primary question that arises from the historical example we have just reviewed is this: Why is the church so silent today?

It is with this question in mind that we turn to the question of *how* the church, based on its biblical and confessional theology, might fulfill its calling to be a sentinel, alert for dangers within its own life and the life of the nation.

Questions for reflection and discussion

1. As you look back on history, when do you feel the church has been too silent in the face of injustice?

2. Can you name historical examples where the state has sought to control the church, that is, to bring it into lock-step with the ideology of the state? Where has the church sought to bring the state under its control?

3. Do you feel that the Church Struggle in Germany in the 1930s and 1940s has any parallel in the United States today? If so, in what respects?

4. Do you feel that there are anti-Muslim or anti-Semitic attitudes in American society? In the church? In your community?

5

Critical Engagement: The Church As Sentinel

In the previous chapter we considered what can happen when the church abandons its commitment to the gospel of Christ to support an alien worldview, in this case an ideology of nationalism and global dominance. The example of the rise of National Socialism is instructive for people of the *church* because it was, for the most part, the "good" people of the church who were either silent in the face of it or active participants in the execution of its policies.

It is against this background that we now turn to the question of how the church, based on its biblical and confessional heritage, might best respond to the claims to global hegemony that are being voiced today. How might it respond to the quasi-religious assumptions behind this self-proclaimed mission to change the world? To which aspects of America's mission to the world should the church say, "Yes, you have our support"? Where, if anywhere, should the church say no? How does our Christian heritage equip us to speak to what many consider to be the singular most important issue of our day? In order to address these questions we must consider the resources of our biblical-confessional heritage, beginning with three key evangelical principles.

Three evangelical principles

The cross is at the center

For the church, the crucified Christ is at the center of life. Over against the wisdom of the world, the church offers "the foolishness" of the cross (1 Cor. 1) as the critical vantage point from which all dimensions of human life are viewed, differentiated, and critiqued. Here the church is not superimposing a doctrinal or ideological overlay onto the rich diversity of life; it is rather expressing a perspective from which the very richness and depth of life can be grasped. When Jesus goes willingly to be crucified before he will allow people to turn him into a god of their own making, he discloses the paradoxical nature of God whose power is found in weakness ("he empties himself, taking the form of a slave," Phil 2:7), whose wisdom is found in that which is foolishness in the eyes of the world.

The cross thus contains an implicit critique of any and all claims to absolute status or loyalty on the part of any person or institution. It is for this reason that from the earliest days Christians have had an uneasy relationship with those who make claims to sovereignty or empire. It confesses that Christ crucified, not Caesar or the Roman Empire or any other empire, is sovereign Lord of all life. It is on the basis of this, its most fundamental creed, that the church is not able to support any nation, should it demand absolute loyalty. This tension between the church and the political authorities characterized the early Christian community under Roman dominion.[1] It erupted in outright confrontation during the period of the Reformation when leaders of the Evangelical movement launched their protest against the abusive power of both church and state. The Refomers called for a return to the heart of the church's proclamation, to the power of the cross expressed in the earliest Christian confession that Jesus Christ is Lord.

The protest of the Reformers was built on the legacy of the Czech leader, Jan Hus (1369–1415). As preacher at the Bethlehem Chapel near the University of Prague, Hus combined a vibrant evangelical spirit with historical knowledge and intellectual rigor, a legacy that remains at the heart of the Moravian Church to this day. His preaching addressed corruption in the church and the unholy alliance between the ecclesiastical and the secular authorities. For his refusal to conform and to cease his efforts to reform the church, Hus was burned at the stake in Constance in 1415. Taking his stand on the freedom of the gospel a century later, Luther declared, "We are all Hussites."

As Jan Hus before him, Luther's affirmation of *sola gratia,* the conviction that people are saved by God's grace alone and not by any human endeavor or institution, means that nothing whatever in the finite world can be justifiably invested with absolute status, neither ideology nor nation nor any form of the church itself. Ultimate authority belongs alone to God, to the living Word that became incarnate in Jesus Christ. Theologian Paul Tillich called this important distinction "the Protestant Principle," because it belonged to the Reformation's protest against every attempt to raise other loyalties, whether persons or institutions, church or state, ideology or empire, to the level of absolute loyalty. Theologian Douglas John Hall has written that the Protestant Principle "was a gospel of liberation from the oppressive authority of finite and conditioned authorities parading as infinite and unconditioned."[2]

This word of judgment on the pretensions of people, systems, and structures is the "critical principle" implied in the cross. It can be summed up in the words of the First Commandment, "You shall have no other gods in place of the one true God." Any oath of allegiance to the country or any "pledge of allegiance to the flag" is thus a secondary or penultimate allegiance. For a Christian the primary allegiance is summed up in Luther's explanation to the First Commandment in his Small Catechism, "We are to fear, love, and trust in God above all things."

What does this mean for our present discussion? At the very least it means that Christians need to be very wary when people claim (chapter 3) that America is destined to privilege, that America is "number one," that the twenty-first century is "the American century." We need to protest when it is claimed that we Americans are the greatest, the most virtuous, the most generous, the "indispensable nation," or that America is "God's country" or that "God is on our side." We can be proud of our country and grateful for its heritage, but we are, in God's eyes, one among many.

The Bible is not a crystal ball

Closely related is the second principle, which states that we dare not confuse the authority of the Word, the Christ, with the authority of the *words* of Scripture. The Bible offers neither a set of codified rules for today nor a blueprint for the world of tomorrow. As noted in chapter 4, it is simply not the purpose of the Bible to either predict or prescribe what is going to happen as nations interact in the twenty-first century. Those who employ the Bible in such a fashion—and they can be heard and seen on many radio and TV programs any day of the week—misuse Scripture, betray its central purpose, and delude people of good will. Consider the role of the biblical prophets. They are not called by God to predict future events; they are called to proclaim God's word of judgment and promise *in the present.* As Rabbi Abraham Heschel wrote in his classic study, *The Prophets:*

> Frightful is the agony of man; no human voice can convey its full terror. Prophecy is the voice that God has lent to the silent agony, a voice to the plundered poor, to the profaned riches of the world. It is a form of living, a crossing point of God and man. God is raging in the prophet's words.[3]

People who bought into the predictions of Hal Lindsay's *The Late Great Planet Earth* were disillusioned when these were not fulfilled. Not to be deterred, his dispensationalist followers simply altered the contemporary referents to the same biblical texts. All of this might be written off as innocuous or innocent were it not for the fact that so large a percentage of Americans—including many members of the U. S. Congress—believe it.

What does this mean for our present discussion? It means that Christians should reject the charlatans who would have us believe that the rise of American power, the events of 9/11, the war in Iraq, and American global hegemony in the twenty-first century belong to God's preordained plan.

The sabbath is made for people

When Jesus said that "the sabbath was made for humankind, not humankind for the sabbath" (Mark 2:27), he was saying, in effect, that every system, every institution, every program is to be judged on the basis of one fundamental criterion, namely, how it serves the well-being of all of God's people. To be sure, some institutions are so corrupt that the church has declared that they have absolutely no redeeming value. The Confessing Church said this about the Nazi regime; the Lutheran World Federation has said this about the system of legalized racism known as apartheid. Yet to make a declaration that a system, a government, an institution, or an ideology is *incompatible* with the gospel of Christ (known as a *status confessionis)*[4] is consistent with the principle that "the sabbath is made for people, not people for the sabbath."

Based upon this principle, it then must be concluded that no single political, economic, or social system can claim to have been ordained by God or sanctioned by the Bible as the one ideal system for humanity. This means that one cannot justifiably assert that, based on the Bible, one particular form of government (e.g., monarchy, parliamentary, democracy) or economy (e.g., socialism, capitalism) has divine preference. Indeed, no direct line leads from the Bible to any social, economic, political, or military issue whatsoever.

It means further that no single form of church-state relationship can claim to be valid for all times and places. Indeed, history has witnessed a considerable variety of expressions of the relationship between the civil authorities and the church. The early church was a distinct minority in the Greco-Roman world. It underwent persecution for refusing to give the state its ultimate loyalty. Under Constantine the church had a privileged position and from that time to the Reformation, church and state struggled for control of political governance. In the East, in Byzantium, church and state were virtually mirror images of each other, forming a close alliance. In his insistence that the church could under certain circumstances justifiably resist the power of the state, Luther contributed to the liberal tradition of institutional separation of church and state. The growth of Western democracies has taken place in the face of a growing pluralism in which a variety of religions have claimed equal status under the law. In the United States the institutional separation of church and state is guaranteed in the First Amendment to the Constitution, which states that "Congress shall make no law respecting an establishment of religion, or prohibiting the free exercise thereof."

What does this mean for our present discussion? It means that even though Christianity is the majority religion in this nation, minority religions should never be subject to the tyranny of the majority. The Constitution guarantees freedom *for* and freedom *from* religion. So Christians should reject every attempt to have their faith subverted by siding exclusively with one political party or elevating one organizational system to an exclusive place above all others, whether that is a system based on free-market capitalism or U. S.-style representative democracy. We need to recognize that other peoples of the world function on different terms than those that characterize our particular society. Christian Scripture provides no detailed blueprint for the ideal earthly society. What God's Word does offer, however, is a vision of a community in which no one is excluded or oppressed, in which each person's dignity is affirmed, and in which all have a share in the fruits of the earth. To guard this vision the church is called to be a sentinel.

The state under God

Keeping in mind these three principles, we now turn to this question: How are Christians, members of the community of the church, to evaluate and respond to the vision of a new world order that is being proposed today? We will begin by asking a question about the understanding of the role of the civil authority from a New Testament vantage point. This will provide a basis for establishing those biblical principles that belong to a normative understanding of the respective roles of church and state. We will ask if there is a Christian right to resist state authority and conclude by calling for the "critical engagement" of the church in the affairs of the state today.

A New Testament perspective

In the New Testament one finds three basic expressions of the relationship of church and state:[5]

1. Obedience to those in authority. The traditional position of obedience to the civil authorities is expressed in the letters of Paul and Peter, and finds its focus in Romans 13: "Let every one be subject to the governing authorities . . ." These and similar verses (e.g., 1 Tim. 2:1, 2; Titus 3:1; 1 Pet. 2:13-17) have shaped the main attitude of Christians toward the state throughout much of history. The government is God's gift to preserve order and maintain the public welfare. Christians give prayerful support and obedience. Church and state are mutually supportive partners in maintaining the welfare of the community. This New Testament view is generally favored in times of relative peace.

2. Critical engagement with those in authority. This ethic represents the dialectical approach of much of the New Testament. It finds its focus in Jesus. Jesus is not a revolutionary (zealot), calling for the overthrow of the Roman government. He permits payment of taxes to Caesar and the Temple hierarchy. He preaches love for the enemy and non-violent resistance to evil. Jesus is no servile subject to those who rule, however. His entire life and ministry are filled with conflict with those in power. He is critical of the abuse of power, wealth, and authority. In the line of the prophets he is scathing in his critique of the religious and civil authorities for their neglect of the poor. In Jesus there is neither an ethic of obedience nor an ethic of violent resistance, but an ethic of critical engagement with those who rule. He provokes the rulers to change, even at the cost of his own life.

3. Resistance to those in authority. The ethic of Christian resistance to totalitarian tendencies by the state finds its focus in Revelation 13. Loyalty to Christ is to be maintained above loyalty to the state and its policies. When the political structures become idolatrous and demonic, the church is called to adopt a position of unqualified resistance. The historical context is one in which Christians refuse to participate in the imperial cult of emperor-state worship under Domitian. Imperial Rome is the anti-Christ, symbolized in the whore, the two beasts, and Babylon. It is to be opposed, not with violence, but with patience, suffering, and non-violent resistance patterned after the Lamb that was slain.

Toward a normative understanding

As mentioned in chapter 1, viewed from the standpoint of Scripture, the civil authority—that is, the state or government—is not simply a law unto itself, autonomous (*auto:* self, *nomos:* law), self-contained, and subject to no external ethical standard or authority. When people speak in our American context of "the separation of church and state," they often think that this means a separation of faith from life, of God from the world of political decision making. This is clearly an untenable position for Christians. Those from the

Christian Right, as well as leaders of mainline Jewish, Christian, and Muslim faith traditions, have been correct in calling for an end to an understanding of "separation" that assumes a radical split between the spiritual dimension of life and the political. Where they are incorrect, however, is when they have presumed that a particular faith perspective has been given a sacred privilege of dictating government policies or that a particular model of social-political organization has been handed down by God.

The state, said Luther, has *not* been given the function of proclaiming the gospel, administering sacraments, or caring for the spiritual needs of the people. This is the God-given role of the church. Just as the state is not called to run the church, the church is not called to govern the political life of society. It is the role of the state to govern equitably based on reason, not to advance a particular religious agenda, even though this separation of roles has been increasingly breached in U. S. politics and policy in recent years. If a Muslim holds a position of political leadership, he or she is God's servant, occupying an office ordained by God. Speaking of rulers, Luther insisted, "better a wise Turk than a foolish Christian."

In all human interactions, including interactions with the state, one is, according to Luther, confronting the living God. One does not infer God's existence or nature by rational argument or empirical observation, as the Scholastics taught. Rather, says Luther, it is "in" and "through" the concreteness of the created world, whether things or people, events or institutions, that God is at least partially revealed. The created world is filled with veils or "masks" of God *(larvae Dei)* that both conceal God's fullness and yet reveal God's presence.

The institutions of the family and the state are masks of God, for through them God "governs and preserves the world." Just as a mother, father, or child is a veil through which one can glimpse God, so also are the kings and ayatollahs, queens, princes, the president, members of Congress, mayors, and local officials. Through them, whether they are Christian or Buddhist or Muslim or atheist, people are confronted by the living God. This position, it might be noted, is in sharp contrast to the contention of some leaders of the Christian right today that political leadership is reserved for Christians alone.

The measure of government, then, is not whether it adopts policies that serve one part of the religious community, but rather its ability to institute laws and ordinances that uphold justice for all people in the community. Here justice is not simply conformity with law; it is the presence of harmony or wholeness, what we sometimes call *salaam* (in Arabic) or *shalom* (in Hebrew), in which everyone has a share in the wealth of the earth, where no one has too much while some have too little, where no one is oppressed and no one is being oppressed. Although the church is not called to rule over the political life, it is called to be a sentinel, to ensure that the state is doing what the state should be doing under God.

Based on this brief overview, it can be at least provisionally concluded that a normative understanding of the relationship of church to state would need to include the following principles:

A Christian's most fundamental loyalty is to God and not to any human institution. Whatever loyalty one expresses to the state, it is subservient to one's ultimate allegiance to God. This is consistent throughout the New Testament.

The state is not an autonomous realm, but is called *by God* to serve the common good. It is to promote peace and justice, ensure equity, and serve its citizens—and all people of the world—with fairness. It preserves law and order and punishes those who offend the public good (Rom. 13:3, 4). The church supports the state and is a partner to the state, but only to the extent that the state fulfills its God-given function of ensuring the common good.

When the state neglects its God-given role as the institution charged with maintaining justice in society, it is the church's task to exercise its role as sentinel and to express its critique through the forms of protest that are available to it.

When the state assumes idolatrous power for itself and demands the ultimate obedience of the people, the state's power must be resisted (Rev. 13). "We must obey God rather than men" (Acts 5:29).

Is there a Christian rationale for resistance?

The short answer is yes. But this is not a simple issue by any means. It is tied to a host of related questions, among them: Under what conditions is resistance justified? Based on which criteria? By what means, violent or non-violent? Who is entitled to make a decision of such magnitude?

As Americans we are probably most familiar with the rationale for resistance to government that was given as we declared our independence from Britain. Schoolchildren across the country have little trouble justifying the decision of the Second Continental Congress to take up arms against the government of George III in order to secure American independence. The right to resistance is enshrined in one of the founding documents of the country, The Declaration of American Independence:

That whenever any Form of Government becomes destructive of these ends, it is the Right of the People to alter or to abolish it, and to institute new Government, laying its foundation on such principles and organizing its powers in such form, as to them shall seem most likely to effect their Safety and Happiness. Prudence, indeed, will dictate that Governments long established should not be changed for light and transient causes; and accordingly all experience hath shewn, that mankind are more disposed to suffer, while evils are sufferable, than to right themselves by abolishing the forms to which they are accustomed. But when a long train of abuses and usurpations, pursuing invariably the same Object evinces a design to reduce them under absolute Despotism, it is their right, it is their duty, to throw off such Government, and to provide new Guards for their future security.

It is significant that, during the last half of the twentieth century, groups in Namibia and South Africa that were engaged in struggles against the *apartheid* Government of South Africa frequently quoted these words from the American Declaration of Independence. The same is true of groups engaged in conflicts against oppressive governments in El Salvador and Guatemala. Since the United States was not viewed as an ally in these struggles, their leaders spoke to the American government in terms they felt would be understood: The very same principle that justified your war for independence against the British in 1776 justifies our struggle against oppressive government today. We ask for your help.

It is generally thought that this appeal to the right of resistance comes exclusively from political theory (e.g., English common law, David Hume). In fact, this right has a much longer tradition in political philosophy. Yet one of its more significant expressions can be found in the evangelical Reformation of the sixteenth century. When Martin Luther stood before Emperor Charles V and said, "I can do no other . . . ," he was saying quite brazenly, "I refuse to obey you or your government." Luther was placed under the emperor's ban for his defiance—in the same way, we might note, that Baptist Roger Williams was banned in Massachusetts, Martin Luther King Jr. was locked up in the Birmingham Jail, and Nelson Mandela was sent to Robben Island.

The example of Dietrich Bonhoeffer is most striking. As the imperial designs and anti-Semitic actions of the Third Reich became more menacing, it became clear for Bonhoeffer that discipleship to

Christ entailed opposition to the Nazi state itself. When, through the intervention of his brother-in-law, Hans von Dohnanyi, he became attached to the nonGestapo-controlled military intelligence unit, Bonhoeffer was not only able to help Jews escape to Switzerland, but was also able to make contact with the Allies in order to enlist their support for a planned *coup* against leaders of the Third Reich. The failed *coup* attempt led to the arrest, imprisonment, and execution of hundreds of people connected to the conspiracy, including Bonhoeffer.

Bonhoeffer had been a pacifist. Yet in the face of the gross violations of human rights perpetrated by the Nazi regime, Bonhoeffer opened the door for an exception. In the late 1930s he departed from his earlier pacifism and stated that, though in normal times a Christian is called to respect the laws of the country, there are exceptional times when obedience to Christ demands that the law be superseded. In a conversation with fellow prisoner, Bonhoeffer provided his justification for taking part in the conspiracy:

> If a madman drives his car on the sidewalk of the Kurfürstendamm [a major boulevard in Berlin], I as a pastor cannot be content to bury the dead and console the families. I must, if I find myself at this place, leap up and prevent the driver from getting away.[6]

Charged with treason, engaging in actions calculated to subvert the authority of the Third Reich, and participating in the resistance movement leading to the plot to take the life of Adolf Hitler, Dietrich Bonhoeffer was hanged by Germany's National Socialist regime at the Flossenberg concentration camp in Bavaria on April 9, 1945.

The case for critical engagement

In light of the foregoing, what is a viable stance for the U. S. church today? One conclusion appears self-evident, namely that, based on Scripture and the Reformation heritage, people of the church have *in principle* a God-given right to oppose policies and practices of the state they consider to contradict God's rule of justice for all people. As Martin Luther King Jr. demonstrated so powerfully, the right of civil disobedience has a long and honored tradition.

Is *violent* resistance an option? No. Under present conditions in the United States today such a response is absolutely *outside* the range of acceptable courses of action. Is this a time for *non-violent* resistance? Forms of non-violent resistance to state policies are always an option; however, people who violate the laws of the land can expect to be punished. Although we are living at a time when the fear of terrorism has led to restrictions on the rights of citizens (as witness the intense debate on the Patriot Act, domestic intelligence gathering, and the limits of Executive authority), it remains a fact that church people, like all citizens, have both the right and the means for protesting the policies and actions of the government.

Of the three options for church-state relationships that have precedent in the New Testament, it is the second, namely "critical engagement," that is most appropriate for our time and place. The option of uncritical obedience, of silence and inaction, would not be helpful, although it is a fact that many people are quite content to do nothing. It needs to be remembered that inaction is not a neutral option; it is an implicit vote of support for the status quo.

On the other hand, if one should disagree with the present direction that America has charted, there are many available means for expressing opposition. One can undertake any number of actions, from calling the White House to writing to congressional representatives, writing books and articles to participating in marches and demonstrations. One can also engage in non-violent acts of civil disobedience, as some have done in protesting the U. S. invasion of Iraq. In taking part in such actions, insofar as they violate the law, one can expect to be detained, fingerprinted, fined, or sentenced to jail time.

Although the range of individual freedom has become narrower because of acts of terror and the government's response to them, we continue to live in an extremely open society. Our freedom to speak out, pro and con, to gather in assembly, to take part in patriotic parades or anti-government protests, is unparalleled in history and unequalled among the nations of the world. It is precisely these freedoms that we are honoring when we speak out, either individually or in community, on the emerging shape of America's role in the world.

Questions for reflection and discussion

1. What does it mean to say that the cross of Christ is judgment on idolatry, whether in personal or national life?

2. Do you feel that the Bible is useful in predicting events in the Middle East? Give reasons for your answer.

3. How do you feel about the present relationship between church and state in the United States today? Are we moving in a constructive direction or are there dangers?

4. Of the three options governing the relationship of church to state described in the New Testament, do you agree that "critical engagement" is the most appropriate for our time and place? Which options, if any, would you rule out?

Epilogue: "Hold On to That Cross!"

The legacy of Gudina Tumsa

I remember him as a good friend and one of the great leaders of the church. With his six-and-a-half-foot stature and large smile, his presence exuded an air of congenial dominance. I recall how he used to look down at me and say, "You're just a *wee* little man," a line he repeated with laughter every time we met.

Gudina Tumsa was from the beginning an evangelist. For him all of life revolved around Jesus Christ. Even as a teen he would walk from village to village in western Ethiopia talking to anyone who would listen about God's amazing, transforming grace through Jesus Christ. If one was looking for the secret of the phenomenal growth in the Ethiopian Evangelical Church Mekane Yesus (EECMY), one need only look to Gudina, the church's general secretary, and to the teacher-evangelists who came under his care.

One of my most indelible remembrances of Gudina came during a time of convulsive unrest in Chile in 1973. We were attending a Lutheran World Federation seminar on the role of the church amid social change. With poor *compesino* families, politicians, and business, agriculture, and church leaders, we had talked for hours about the contours of a vision for a more just and egalitarian society in Chile.

On the last day of the seminar Gudina and I went for a walk through the streets of Santiago, just to talk and perhaps to purchase a memento or two. But on that final day I found that Gudina's thoughts were fixed, not on Chile but on his own country, Ethiopia.

He was preoccupied with what was on the horizon at home as the old feudal order under Emperor Haile Selassie was about to give way to the revolutionary Marxist government of Mengistu Haile Miriam. Aware of the fact that both he and the congregations of the EECMY needed to be better prepared for what was coming, Gudina looked to the Chilean example for guidance.

Gudina had a vision for his country not unlike the vision that we had for Chile—or the vision of *shalom* that the prophets held up to Israel in biblical times. Inspired by the teachings of Jesus about the kingdom of God, he envisioned a land in which all were welcome—women and men, children and grown-ups, rich and poor, Jews and Gentiles, the sick, the blind, the disabled, and all had a share in the wealth of the earth.

Gudina also had an exhilarating sense of the freedom of the Christian, as expressed in the words of Martin Luther, "A Christian is the most free lord of all, subject to none. A Christian is the most dutiful servant of all, subject to all." He felt completely liberated by the gospel. If God held him secure for all eternity, he reasoned, there was no reason to fear any person or institution today. He had been inspired by the example of Martin Luther King Jr., who powerfully expressed Luther's sense of being "the most free lord of all, subject to none," on April 3, 1968, the day before an assassin's bullet ended his life:

> I just want to do God's will. And He's allowed me to go up to the mountain. And I've looked over. And I've seen the promised land. I may not get there with you. But I want you to know tonight, that we, as a people, will get to the promised land. And I'm happy, tonight. I'm not worried about anything. I'm not fearing any man. Mine eyes have seen the glory of the coming of the Lord.[1]

Convinced that there was an inherent ecumenical thrust at the heart of the Lutheran tradition, Gudina brought his church into a position of leadership in the ecumenical movement. In that same freedom he moved out to engage Muslims in interfaith dialogue and joined with people of many faith traditions in undertaking common action on behalf of people affected by famine. On the other side of the equation, Gudina felt constrained by the gospel to be "the most dutiful servant of all, subject to all." It was that calling to follow Christ, to take up the cross of discipleship, to be "servant of all" that was to become his legacy in the years to come.

As Gudina and I walked in Santiago together, the streets were relatively peaceful. But it was a tense time in Chile, and we were cautioned not to go out alone. Efforts to destabilize the young presidency of Salvador Allende Gossens and create general chaos in the country were evident on every hand. Although the churches, Roman Catholic, as well as Pentecostal, Lutheran, Anglican, Presbyterian, Methodist, and Baptist, were hopeful that the new government would work to change conditions for the poorest sectors, it was evident that the forces of business and industry, as well as the military, were determined to bring the socialist government down.

Gudina and I stopped at a kiosk where I purchased a crude wooden crucifix, which still hangs today on the wall of my home study, reminding me of that day. As we walked away, Gudina and I found ourselves suddenly cordoned off by heavily armed police, then pushed up against the kiosk by a burst from a water cannon. A policeman yelled, "Vamoose," and we hightailed it through the streets of Santiago, running from water cannons, police barricades, and barking dogs—and me clutching the crucifix.

When we stopped to catch our breath, Gudina, dripping wet, looked at me and laughed. But then he said words that I will never forget: "Hold on to that cross, Paul, hold on to Jesus. Don't ever let go."

Three months later the government of Chile was overthrown and the president murdered. The ruthless, oppressive rule of General August Pinochet began. Gudina returned to Ethiopia to face a more difficult challenge than he had expected. The Marxist revolution was about to engulf the country. Years of great suffering for the people, including the communities of faith would follow, culminating in the "Red Terror" of 1978–79 in which many leaders of the Ethiopian religious community were imprisoned, tortured, and killed.

On July 28, 1979, following an evening worship service at the congregation of the Urael Mekane Yesus Church in Addis Ababa, Gudina and his wife, Tsahai Tolessa, were picked up on the street by the government's security forces. Tsahai was released. Gudina was physically abused and executed.

Who is Jesus Christ for us today?

When the church takes part in a discussion on the future of America and its role in helping to shape the future of the world community, it participates in a discussion quite similar to that in which Gudina and I engaged during that gathering over thirty years ago. Based on Gudina's vision, his sense of freedom in Christ, and his readiness to pay the cost of discipleship through his ministry to others, I have three observations about the present challenge to the church.

1. A vision of the kingdom

For a Christian in America today it is not enough to simply protest the direction and policies of the government. People of the church are called to participate with others in developing a constructive alternative. They offer neither a blueprint for the ideal society nor an action plan for achieving it. The Bible offers no special wisdom on the technicalities of trade or the subtleties of geopolitical strategy. Like others, Christians need to use their God-given reason and common sense, their knowledge of the disciplines, and their experience of the past.

Yet Christians do have a vision, which Scripture expresses in the term *kingdom of God*. This does not refer either to an ideal society or to a model of social organization devised by Christian people. Rather, it expresses God's dominion over all dimensions of personal and social life. The power and meaning of God's rule has become manifest in history in the life, death, and resurrection of Christ. Its "signs" are discerned in the transformation of life through the power of God's grace. In such moments (for instance, taking in a homeless family, hearing the word of forgiveness for a wrong committed, risking one's life for a stranger), one is able to glimpse, however partially, a vision of the kingdom's fulfillment at the end of history. Although no amount of engagement by Christians, critical or otherwise, will usher in the fullness of the kingdom, Christians are called to hold up the vision and participate in those events that point to its coming.

Christians work to establish a social order in which genuine justice and peace prevail. Believing that all people are created in the image of God, they are committed to affirming human dignity and rights in every dimension of social life. They carry with them an inclusive vision, one in which no one is an island, where all are part of the main. Their vision for America is intrinsically linked to their vision for the world.

Martin Luther King Jr. lived this global vision. In spite of protests by colleagues that he should stick to the struggle for civil rights in the United States, King expressed himself publicly about the Vietnam War and about apartheid in South Africa. It was all of a single piece; justice was one. His vision for America was part of his vision for the world. His God was the creator of heaven and earth, the God who loved the world, the God of justice, not for some people, but for *all* people. For him Christ died, not for a single race or class or nation, but for the whole human family. For King it was the vision of God's rule that needed to take form, however sporadically and imperfectly, in the life of the world.

When Hurricane Katrina devastated the U. S. Gulf Coast in 2005, the entire country—the entire world—was given a glimpse of the "other America," poor, black, powerless. The images of bodies floating in the polluted waters, old people dying in the halls of the Superdome, and mothers and fathers weeping because they had nothing to feed their children, were heart wrenching. Although the overwhelming response to the disaster, however delayed, brought out the best in the American people, the catastrophe itself raised a very simple and direct question: Are we one society or two? Are we willing to tolerate a reality that is so far removed from the vision to which we pledge allegiance—a vision of "one nation, under God, indivisible, with liberty and justice for all"? For the church a second question follows naturally upon the first: Are we committed to a vision of *one world*, under God, indivisible, with liberty and justice for all?

2. Baptismal freedom

What we need today is a national dialogue about our country and its role in the world. What are our priorities? How do they mesh with the priorities of others? I contend that it is in the church's colleges, seminaries, and assemblies—but especially in the congregations—that people of differing social, economic, and political stripes are able, in light of God's Word, to address the most difficult issues that are before the community, the nation, and the world. Are we ready for that? Are we secure enough? Are we free enough?

The presiding bishop of the Evangelical Lutheran Church in America (ELCA), Rev. Mark Hanson, in 2004 lamented the typical response to his public statements, "Bishop Hanson, by what right do you speak on Iraq? You do not speak for me. Why don't you stick to something you should know something about, like telling people about Jesus?" In response, he stated, "I always begin at the same place, the baptismal font. I speak by virtue of my baptismal calling. I hope you are speaking on the basis of yours."[2] To those who reject in principle the role of the pastor to speak out on the burning issues of the day, the bishop quotes the ELCA Constitution, to wit:

Consistent with the faith and practice of the ELCA, every ordained minister shall . . . conduct public worship [and] speak publicly to the world in solidarity with the poor and oppressed, calling for justice and proclaiming God's love for the world.[3]

Offices for church and society in all the mainline churches have guidelines to help equip the local congregation and its pastor to speak on matters of public policy, especially when the dignity and rights of individuals are being violated or when it is believed that the country itself is moving in the wrong direction. The congregation, through open forums, study groups, and social-concern committees, remains one of the most potentially creative communities in society.

In his article, "Let's Talk Politics," Martin Marty pleads for free and open debate on the critical issues of the day. He asks:

[I]f we regard government and thus politics—which can mean "regard for the *polis,* the human city"—as being "ordained by God," can we not in our parishes find some ways to discuss issues and there subject each other's commitments and opinions to some sort of biblical and theological analyses?[4]

As the church, we have tremendous resources for pursuing such a discussion. But are we free enough to do so?

3. The cost of discipleship

During the final days of his life, Gudina Tumsa referred indirectly to the one person who had been the model for his ministry, German pastor Dietrich Bonhoeffer:

As someone [Bonhoeffer] has said, when a person is called to follow Christ, that person is called to die. It means a redirection of the purpose of life, that is, death to one's own wishes and personal desires and finding the greatest satisfaction in living for and serving the one who died for us and was raised from death (2 Corinthians 5:13, 14).[5]

Bonhoeffer was encouraged by colleagues to remain in America in 1939, where he held a teaching position at Union Theological Seminary in New York. He had been emotionally torn about leaving, but finally wrote to Reinhold Niebuhr:

> I have come to the conclusion that I have made a mistake in coming to America. I must live through this difficult period of our national history with the Christian people of Germany. I will have no right to participate in the reconstruction of Christian life in Germany after the war if I do not share the trials of this time with my people.[6]

Gudina was similarly given an opportunity to leave Ethiopia in 1979. Through the mediation of Lutheran World Federation leaders, Tanzanian president Julius Nyerere agreed to arrangements whereby Gudina and his family would be transported to safety in Tanzania. But when he heard about the agreement, Gudina responded adamantly:

> Here is my church and my congregation. How can I, as a church leader, leave my flock at this moment of trial? I have again and again pleaded with my pastors to stay on. "Christ died for all that those who live should no longer live for themselves but for him who died for them and was raised again."[7]

Although the situation in Bonhoeffer's Germany and Gudina's Ethiopia might bear little comparison with the state of America today, the demands of discipleship remain the same. One question their legacy wills to us is this: How can we who are committed to Christ and his church—and who are also committed to our country—help steer the country onto a responsible path that will bring its immense resources to bear on the building of a more just and peaceful world?

Their legacy also raises this question: What is the role of the Christian when the policies of the state diverge from the church's discernment of God's will? For Bonhoeffer the answer is, in obedience to God, to act in freedom, but with responsibility for the sake of the other, even if this means incurring guilt and challenging the laws of the civil order. For Gudina the role of the Christian is in principle the same. There is, under normal circumstances, an obligation to obey the law. But this obligation is not absolute. It holds only to a certain point. As Gudina wrote:

> It has been stated that a Christian is a citizen of a given country and as such under the laws and policies of that country. Because he is under the laws of the country of which he is a citizen, it is his duty to pray for the peace of that country and cooperate with his fellow citizens for its well-being. The only limitation to his cooperation or obedience to the laws of his country is if he is commanded to act contrary to the law of God ["We must obey God rather than men,"] (Acts 5:29).[8]

For Gudina, the Christian's role in such a situation is one of critical engagement and, if necessary, resistance:

> A responsible Christian does not aggravate any situation and thereby court martyrdom. . . . To be a Christian is not to be a hero to make history for oneself. A Christian goes as a lamb to be slaughtered only when he/she knows that this is in complete accord with the will of God who has called him to his service.[9]

Too often the church has avoided taking any stand at all, be it during the Holocaust in Europe or the persecution of the church in

Ethiopia. I recall times when as a pastor I was part of this conspiracy of silence, when Cambodia was being bombed in 1969 and when the inhabitants of the Salvadoran village of El Mozote were systematically annihilated by the U. S.-trained Atacatl Battalion in 1981. As this nation built up its military forces in Vietnam, I was among a great number who felt that U. S. leaders were pursuing the wrong course. But in the early days I was like the dozing sentinel on the city wall who failed to sound the alarm.

I thank God that the burden of the past, including my own silence and inaction, has been lifted by the power of God's grace. I am grateful that this same grace is able to free us to become sentinels, to speak out and to act at this critical moment in history. In spite of problems at home and abroad, America remains a unique land of freedom and opportunity. Even though the restrictions that have been imposed since 9/11 mean that its borders are not as porous as they once were, this country remains one of the few that continues to welcome to its shores a great many people seeking freedom from political oppression and economic hardship. For them the vision of the original Americans—and the vision of John Winthrop—remains both promise and challenge.

Just as the founding fathers and mothers gathered together to chart a course for the new nation, so are we today called to gather for the purpose of sharing our thoughts and dreams about the future of America and its role in the world. Although we are, gratefully, not in the situation of Dietrich Bonhoeffer or Gudina Tumsa, we can nevertheless learn from them and their commitment to keep faith with the same Lord of church and world. For those of us who would follow Christ in America today, the question is this: Are we willing to take the path of discipleship and are we ready to pay the cost? Or, as Bonhoeffer put it, "Who really is Jesus Christ for us today?"

Suggestions for Engagement

Begin a study group on America's role in the world and how the church, out of its biblical and theological tradition, can best address this issue.

Gather concerned laypeople with the pastor of your congregation to ask how the congregation can address issues in a mutual and constructive way.

Reflect on and study the common roots of Judaism, Islam, and Christianity with people from those faith traditions. These Web sites may be helpful in that task: http://www.cair-net.org/; http://www.masnet.org/; http://www.mpac.org/

Visit Jerusalem with a group from your area. Obtain speakers for your group and participate in events sponsored by Partners for Peace, http://www.partnersforpeace.com, Holy Land Christian Ecumenical Foundation, http://www.hcef.org/hcef/, Churches for Middle East Peace, http://www.cmep.org, Americans for Middle East Understanding, http://www.ameu.org/, Evangelical Lutheran Church in Jerusalem and the Holy Land, http://www.holyland-lutherans.org/, and the International Center of Bethlehem, http://www.annadwa.org/. Support these groups financially.

Take part in marches and demonstrations that peacefully express your opinion on the war in Iraq and the agenda of which it is a part.

Encourage your representatives to support the United Nations. Support the United Nations Children Fund (UNICEF) http://www. unicef.org/; Join a local chapter of the United Nations Association, http://www.unausa.org/; apply for an assignment with the UN, http://www.un.org/Depts/icsc/vab; become a UN election monitor.

Participate in and support the work of the Council for a Parliament of the World's Religions at http://www.cpwr.org. Get on their mailing list, find a speaker for your congregation, join the Partner City Program which the Council operates in seventy cities.

Express your concerns by letter and e-mail to your congressional representatives. Letters from groups within the congregation (speaking only for themselves, of course) are well received.

Call the White House at (202) 456-1111 or e-mail at president@whitehouse.gov and leave a message for the president. All messages are tabulated and conveyed.

Make a common statement on concerns—for instance, globalization, the war on terror, the Iraq war—that are shared with friends in your sister synod or sister congregation abroad.

If a political party asks for the directory of your church for the purpose of soliciting support from church members, refuse.

When any religion is attacked verbally or in writing, find a way to protest.

Notes

Chapter 1

1. What has become known as "the Bush Doctrine" is defined in the speech by President George W. Bush at West Point on June 1, 2002 (http://www.whitehouse.gov/news/releases/2002/06/20020601-3.html) and in his State of the Union speech in 2004 (http://www.whitehouse.gov/news/releases/2004/01/20040120-7.html). It is also developed in the National Security Strategy (http://www.whitehouse.gov/nsc/nss.html) that was adopted on September 17, 2002.

2. See http://globalization.about.com/library/weekly/aa073098.htm; also Desmond Tutu, *No Future Without Forgiveness* (Garden City, N.Y.: Doubleday, 1997), 152, 153.

3. See Martin Luther, *Temporal Authority: To What Extent It Should Be Obeyed (1523)*, in *Luther's Works, American Edition*, ed. Walter I. Brandt, vol. 45 (Philadelphia: Fortress Press, 1962.)

4. "Sentinel, what of the night?" (Isa. 21:11); see also, e.g., 1 Sam. 14:16; 2 Kgs. 9:17; Ps. 127:1, Jer. 31:6, Ezek. 33:2, 6.

Chapter 2

1. James Wilson, *The Earth Shall Weep: A History of Native America* (New York: Grove Press, 1998), 8.

2. The Greeks used the word *telos* to describe the intrinsic aim or goal of things, that which provides an inner directedness, or purpose. For Aristotle the most important of his four "causes" or "reasons" for a thing is the purpose for which it was made. Thus, the goal or *telos* of an acorn is to become an oak tree. In the New Testament life itself has an inner *telos;* all of history moves toward a future fulfillment at the end of time. But is there a *telos* for groups within history, for nations? One thing is clear, and that is that most nations articulate such a purpose for their national existence. Groups that move history are driven by sense of destiny, that is, by the goals toward which they strive and purposes they

seek to fulfill. Sometimes this sense of destiny is termed a "vocational consciousness." Vocation, in this context, does not mean job or occupation, but a sense of calling *(vocatio)*. In varying degrees of awareness and motivating power, historical groups are held together internally and driven to act externally by a particular sense of calling.

3. It is something of a stretch to speak of "a" Puritan vision. As Perry Miller makes clear in his classic book, *The American Puritan: Their Prose and Poetry* (Garden City, N.Y.: Doubleday, 1956), there were many interpretations of God's will for the new nation. Though Puritans, like the Pilgrims, were Calvinist, and had a vision of God's sovereignty over all life, it cannot be said that they were democratic and open to innovation. Still, as heirs of the traditions of the Reformation and Renaissance humanism, they were committed to tolerance, equality, and the use of reason in matters of society. Here the term will refer primarily to those who adopted John Winthrop's vision for the nation.

4. John Winthrop, "A Model of Christian Charity," in Miller, *The American Puritan,* 83.

5. Ibid.

6. Ibid., 84.

7. Robert Bellah, "Civil Religion in America," *Dædalus: Journal of the American Academy of Arts and Sciences 96,* no. 1 (Winter 1967): 1-21. Available also online at http://hirr.hartsem.edu/Bellah/articles_5.htm.

8. Richard A. Horsley, *Jesus and Empire: The Kingdom of God and the New World Disorder* (Minneapolis: Fortress Press, 2003), 1.

9. Ironically, it was the same story of liberation from bondage in Egypt that inspired the African American quest for liberation. As Horsley notes in *Jesus and Empire* (ibid., 1, 2), although not permitted to learn to read, African American slaves, when they heard the biblical stories of the Israelites' exodus from bondage and the promised land to which God guided them, fantasized escaping from slavery and "goin' over Jordan" to the promised land of freedom.

10. Available online at http://www.usa-presidents.info/union/mckinley-2.html

11. Charles Beard, *An Economic Interpretation of the Constitution of the United States* (New York: The Free Press, 1913).

12. Reinhold Niebuhr, *The Irony of American History* (New York: Charles Scribner's Sons, 1954).
13. Peter Storey, "Every War Is a Civil War," *Duke University Divinity School News*, Feb. 28, 2003. http://www.dukenews.duke.edu/2003/02/storey0203.html

Chapter 3

1. Madeleine Albright, "If we have to use force, it is because we are America. We are the indispensable nation. We stand tall. We see further into the future." Available online at http://www.brainyquote.com/quotes/authors/m/madeleine_albright.html
2. Gary Dorrien, *Imperial Designs: Neoconservatism and the New Pax Americana* (New York: Routledge, 2004), 224.
3. Mark Juergensmeyer, *Terror in the Mind of God: The Global Rise of Religious Violence* (Berkeley: University of California Press, 2000), 124–28.
4. The National Security Strategy of the United States of America, September 17, 2002 (http://www.whitehouse.gov/nsc/nss.html).
5. Charles Krauthammer, "Universal Dominion: Toward a Unipolar World," *National Interest 18* (Winter 1989), 48–49; see also Krauthammer, "The Unipolar Moment," *Foreign Affairs 70* (1991), 23.
6. Ben Wattenberg, *First Universal Nation: Leading Indicators and Ideas about the Surge of America in the 1990s* (New York: Free Press, 1991), 20, 24.
7. Joshua Muravchik, *Exporting Democracy: Fulfilling America's Destiny* (Washington, D.C.: American Enterprise Institute, 1991), 227.
8. There is some debate among neoconservatives and others on the sequence in which governments of the Middle East should be replaced. General Wesley Clark, Supreme Commander of NATO and a candidate for the 2004 Democratic presidential nomination, has said he was informed in the aftermath of 9/11 that the Pentagon had a five-year plan to overthrow the governments of Iraq, Syria, Lebanon, Libya, Iran, Somalia, and Sudan. Columnist Charles Krauthammer has called for the overthrow of Afghanistan, Syria, and Iraq. Former Israeli Prime Minister, Benjamin Netanyahu, argued for the inclusion of Hamas and Hezbollah in the list. Others argued that North Korea,

Saudi Arabia, and Egypt be added. See Dorrien, *Imperial Design,* 243–44.

9. National Security Strategy, http://www.whitehouse.gov/nsc/nss.html.

Chapter 4

1. See especially Doris L. Bergen, *Twisted Cross: The German Christian Movement during the Third Reich* (Chapel Hill: University of North Carolina Press, 1996), and Robert P. Ericksen and Susannah Heschel, eds., *Betrayal: German Churches and the Holocaust* (Minneapolis: Fortress Press, 1999).

2. http://www.whitehouse.gov/news/releases/2002/05/20020523-2.html

3. Besides Ericksen and Heschel, eds., *Betrayal,* see also the DVD "Theologians Under Hitler" (2005), produced by Vital Visuals, Inc., 16 Brewster Lane., Oak Ridge, TN 37830.

4. Robert P. Ericksen, "Assessing the Heritage: German Protestant Theologians, Nazis, and the 'Jewish Question,'" in Ericksen and Heschel, eds., *Betrayal,* 23.

5. Ibid., 24.

6. Ibid., 25.

7. Ibid., 26.

8. Ibid., 35.

9. The Church of the Prussian Union was an amalgam of Lutheran and Reformed congregations dating back to their forced merger in 1817 under Friedrich Wilhelm III.

10. The Barmen Declaration, available online at http://medg.lcs.mit.edu/doyle/personal/enters/hermann/declaration.html.

11. Ibid.

12. Conversation with Eberhard Bethge, April 1984, Bonhoeffer Conference, Seattle, Washington.

13. Dietrich Bonhoeffer, quoted in Ericksen and Heschel, eds., *Betrayal,* 126.

14. Ibid., 127.

15. http://www.confessingchrist.net, the Web site of "Confessing Christ" of the United Church of Christ; see Statement of Principles.

16. Conrad Braaten, "An Elephant in the Sanctuary: Engaging Issues of War and Peace," *Congregations* (Fall 2003), 24.

17. Ibid., 25.

18. Dietrich Bonhoeffer *Werke 10: Barcelona, Berlin, Amerika, 1928–1931* (Munich: Christian Kaiser Verlag, 1991), 385–86.

19. In her article, "Yesterday and Today: Nazis and the Righteous Right," writer Donna Glee Williams describes the bitterness among the populace at the perceived injustice of the Versailles Treaty in Germany of the 1920s and 1930s that led to the rise of nationalism combined with a drastic curtailment of civil rights. She claims that this sense of being wronged has a parallel in the feelings of many Americans who experienced the terror attacks of 9/11 as a "cultural assault on our inner landscape," on our sense of pride as Americans. "Just as deep resentment was transformed into extreme nationalism in Germany, it has also occasioned a similar reaction in America today." CommonDreams.org, May 2, 2005, http://www.commondreams.org/cgi-bin/print.cgi?file=/views05/0502-33.htm.

20. Bill Moyers, "There Is No Tomorrow," *Minneapolis Star Tribune* (30 Jan. 2005). Available online at http://www.truthout.org/cgi-bin/artman/exec/view.cgi/38/8664.

21. Ibid.

22. Bill Moyers, "Welcome to Doomsday," *New York Review of Books 52,* no. 5 (24 March 2005). Available online at http://nature.berkeley.edu/pipermail/espm-forum/2005-March/000000.html. Moyers felt constrained to add, "I'm not making this up."

23. Barbara R. Rossing, *The Rapture Exposed: The Message of Hope in the Book of Revelation* (Boulder, Colo.: Westview Press, 2004), 48. In this excellent book, Rossing, professor of New Testament at the Lutheran School of Theology in Chicago, has undertaken a scholarly analysis of the dispensationalist worldview. This is important reading for anyone who wants to learn about the history of the dispensationalist phenomenon as well as its profound implications for the shape of U. S. foreign policy today.

24. Moyers, "Welcome to Doomsday," http://nature.berkeley.edu/pipermail/espm-forum/2005-March/000000.html.

25. These remarks by Graham, Robertson, and Falwell are available online at http://www.religioustolerance.org/reac_ter18b.htm.

26. Moyers, "There Is No Tomorrow," http://www.truthout.org/cgi-bin/artman/exec/view.cgi/38/8664.

27. Rossing, *The Rapture Exposed*, 62.

Chapter 5

1. See the excellent books by Richard A. Horsley, *Religion and Empire: People, Power, and the Life of the Spirit*, Facets (Minneapolis Fortress Press, 2003), and *Jesus and Empire: The Kingdom of God and the New World Disorder* (Minneapolis: Fortress Press, 2003).

2. Douglas John Hall, *Thinking the Faith: Christian Theology in a North American Context* (Minneapolis: Fortress Press, 1989), 262.

3. Abraham J. Heschel, *The Prophets* (New York: Harper and Row, 1962), 5.

4. *Status confessionis* refers to (literally) a "state of confession" that ensues when, in place of the sovereign God and the freedom of the gospel, an institution or belief system is seen to demand ultimate loyalty. At such times a Christian's freedom in matters of adiaphora (those things not expressly commanded or forbidden) becomes limited. Such an institution or belief system is to be rejected, not simply because it violates social mores or laws, but because it contradicts the faith itself. See Article X, Formula of Concord, Solid Declaration in *The Book of Concord*, ed. Robert Kolb and Timothy J. Wengert (Minneapolis: Fortress Press, 2000), 515, 516.

5. See Walter Pilgrim's excellent study, *Uneasy Neighbors: Church and State in the New Testament, Overtures to Biblical Theology* (Minneapolis: Fortress Press, 1999). The overview of New Testament perspectives on church and state offered here is indebted to Pilgrim.

6. André Dumas, *Dietrich Bonhoeffer: Theologian of Reality* (London: SCM Press, 1971), 55.

Epilogue

1. Available online at http://www.windsofchange.net/archives/002576.php

2. Bishop Hanson made these remarks at the 2004 Cynthia Wedel lecture, "Probing Questions in the Midst of Peacemaking," sponsored by The Churches' Center for Theology and Public Policy in Washington, D.C. on October 22, 2004.

3. Constitution, Bylaws, and Continuing Resolutions of the ELCA, Provision 7.31.12, quoted by Hanson in his lecture, "Probing Questions in the Midst of Peacemaking."

4. Martin Marty, "Let's Talk Politics," *The Lutheran* (October 2004); http://www.thelutheran.org/article/article_buy.cfm?article_id=1433.

5. Gudina Tumsa, *Witness and Discipleship: Leadership of the Church in Multi-Ethnic Ethiopia in a Time of Revolution,* 11. Published by The Gudina Tumsa Foundation, P.O. Box 4003, Addis Ababa, Ethiopia.

6. Benjamin A. Reist, *The Promise of Bonheffer* (New York: J. B. Lippincott, 1969), 28.

7. Øyvind M. Eide, *Revolution & Religion in Ethiopia: The Growth and Persecution of the Mekane Yesus Church, 1974–1985* (Addis Ababa: Addis Ababa University Press, 2000), 176.

8. Tumsa, 12.

9. Ibid., 9.

Bibliography

Avram, Wes, ed. *Anxious about Empire: Theological Essays on the New Global Realities.* Grand Rapids, Mich.: Brazos Press, 2004.

Berger, Doris L. *Twisted Cross: The German Christian Movement in the Third Reich.* Chapel Hill: University of North Carolina Press, 1996.

Chomsky, Noam. *Hegemony or Survival: America's Quest for Global Dominance.* New York: Henry Holt and Company, 2003.

Dorrien, Gary J. *Imperial Designs: Neoconservatism and the New Pax Americana.* New York: Routledge, 2004.

Ericksen, Robert P., and Susannah Heschel, eds. *Betrayal: German Christians and the Holocaust.* Minneapolis: Fortress Press, 1999.

Haas, Richard N. *The Opportunity: America's Moment to Alter History's Course.* New York: Public Affairs, 2005.

Horsley, Richard A. *Jesus and Empire: The Kingdom of God and the New World Disorder.* Minneapolis: Fortress Press, 2003.

Horsley, Richard A. *Religion and Empire: People, Power, and the Life of the Spirit.* Facets. Minneapolis: Fortress Press, 2003.

Jewett, Robert, and John Shelton Lawrence. *Captain America and the Crusade against Evil: The Dilemma of Zealous Nationalism.* Grand Rapids, Mich.: Wm. B. Eerdmans, 2003.

Moe-Lobeda, Cynthia D. *Public Church: For the Life of the World*. Lutheran Voices. Minneapolis: Augsburg Fortress, 2004.

Muravchik, Joshua. *Exporting Democracy: Fulfilling America's Destiny*. Washington, D.C.: The AEI Press, 1992.

Pilgrim, Walter E. *Uneasy Neighbors: Church and State in the New Testament*. Overtures to Biblical Theology. Minneapolis: Fortress Press, 1999.

Rasmussen, Larry L. *Dietrich Bonhoeffer: Reality and Resistance*. New York: Abingdon Press, 1972.

Rossing, Barbara R. *The Rapture Exposed: The Message of Hope in the Book of Revelation*. Boulder, Colo.: Westview Press, 2004.

Sizer, Stephen. *Christian Zionism: Road-Map to Armageddon*. Leister, England: InterVarsity Press, 2004.

Stumme, John R., and Robert W. Tuttle, eds. *Church and State: Lutheran Perspectives*. Minneapolis: Fortress Press, 2003.

Wallis, Jim. *God's Politics: Why the Right Gets It Wrong and the Left Doesn't Get It, A New Vision for Faith and Politics in America*. San Francisco: HarperSanFrancisco, 2005.

Wind, Renate. *Dietrich Bonhoeffer: A Spoke in the Wheel*. Grand Rapids, Mich.: Eerdman's Publishing Company, 1992.